Loving
Alasdair

For Robert

Loving Alasdair

the 39 years
of my life with
Alasdair Gray

A MEMOIR

May Hooper

Published 2024 by Voices
an imprint of
Lexus Ltd
47 Broad Street, Glasgow G40 2QW, Scotland
© May Hooper

Cover image and sketch of Alasdair Gray by May Hooper
Photographs of Alasdair Gray were taken by May Hooper
The drawing of Alasdair Gray on page 70 courtesy of
    Ranald MacColl
Cover design and Glasgow drawings by Elfreda Crehan

British Library Cataloguing in Publication Data.
A catalogue record for this book is available from the British
Library.
ISBN: 9781904737667

Printed and bound in Europe by Pulsio SARL

www.lexusforlanguages.co.uk

VOICES brings you lives of remarkable people. What lies at the heart is not the glitz of celebrity but the vastness of human experience. Made into words.

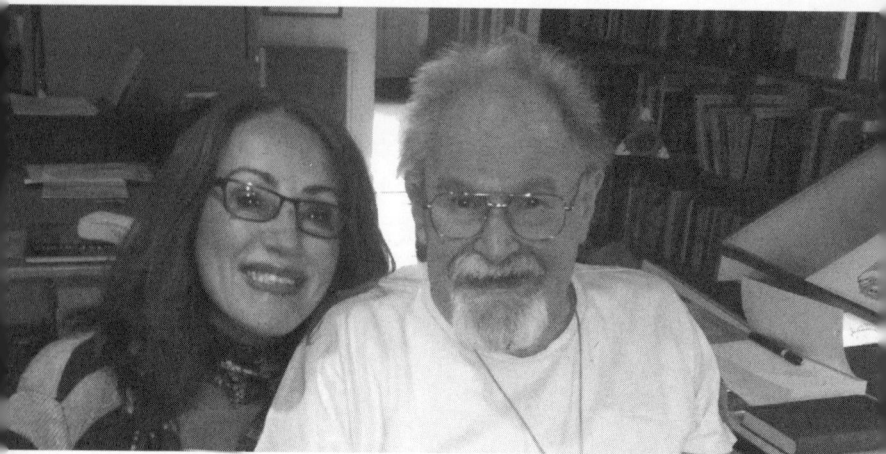

Contents

Part Three

Part Four

Preface

from Ulrike Seeberger
Nuremberg
Germany

Hello May

I have heard from Lexus Books that you are writing a memoir of your life with Alasdair Gray. I thought you might like to hear some of my memories of him.

I knew Alasdair well. He was the one who was instrumental in getting me into literary translations. The German publisher Aufbau bought (but never published) *Unlikely Stories Mostly*, and he remembered that I had translated some of the stories and Bernd Rullkötter, his 'tame translator' recommended me to Aufbau. I worked very closely with Alasdair on the translations of *Unlikely Stories*. I got to know him just after the publication of *Lanark* at the birthday party of his then partner, Bethsy Gray (who had been married to someone also called Gray).

I probably was the last person to receive a Christmas card from Alasdair. He always wrote my address in a rather peculiar fashion and German posties don't all seem to be able to read 'joined-up' writing. So his very nice (always designed by him) Christmas card arrived in 2020, about three weeks after his death.

He was one of the kindest people I have ever known. And I learned a lot about prose rhythms and word colours from him. And he was one of the best-read people I have ever met. He had a way of incorporating what he read into his system of thinking and was able to quote Goethe and Thomas Mann off the cuff.

I have very fond memories of Alasdair, some quirky, some very funny, some not so funny. His visit with Morag here in Nuremberg in May 2002 was at a very difficult time for both of them. They were a bit like babes in the wood, seemed lost in the world, and both drinking a bit too much for their health. They stayed with me for a whole week and several empty vodka bottles were found in their room when they left. And Morag at that time had given up eating altogether.

Alasdair's visit was part of a programme organised by the Nuremberg twinning department inviting writers and journalists from the city's numerous twin cities. Apart from a very well received reading from *Unlikely Stories Mostly*, Alasdair kept busy drawing portraits of all his fellow visitors. Unfortunately most of these impromptu portraits were taken home to the other twin cities. So Nuremberg missed out on a really interesting compilation of drawings.

Shortly afterwards Colin Beattie commissioned Alasdair to paint the mural in the Òran Mór and that really saved his life.

sunny greetings from Nuremberg

Uli

PART ONE

Part One

Here we were again

Here we were again, hurtling through the city in the back of an ambulance, and this time I had serious doubts if Alasdair would pull through. It was uncomfortable, strapped into the unforgiving, bone-jarring seat, but it stimulated my senses, making me more vigilant. You see, I'd come to think of Alasdair as some sort of real-life smarty-pants superhero. But as I glanced over at his face – bluish grey and trembling lips – I had to admit he looked anything but invincible. We'd been in ambulances together more times than I cared to remember, and each ride left me a bundle of nerves, while he, annoyingly calm, would whisper, "I'll be fine – no need to worry."

Two weeks earlier, he'd managed to perform the incredible feat of severing an artery on his face while shaving. Blood sprayed everywhere, as it tends to do when Alasdair Gray was involved. Most people would find such a mishap utterly implausible, but then again Alasdair was anything but ordinary. He should never have been shaving himself, he had great difficulty moving his arms above shoulder height. Why did they let him do it?

I could usually control the bleeding from his not infrequent self-inflicted shaving mishaps, but that day had been different. I had rushed to his flat in response to the call from Stef, his panicked assistant. The scene was reminiscent of a horror movie, and even the hospital doctors had struggled to control the arterial spray. You could say I'd grown accustomed to our hospital visits, but it wasn't a part of life I particularly relished. Still, something about this ambulance ride now felt unlike the others.

As the ambulance bounced along – albeit not quickly enough for my liking – I couldn't help but steal a worried glance at the man who, just moments ago, had tried to reassure me. But now he was gasping for breath, his blood pressure had been unrecordable before the ambulance's arrival (I keep a first-aid kit and a BP machine in my flat – old nursing habits die hard, after all), and his dry, blue lips could barely form words. Holding him close, I had dialled 999, my heart pounding, praying they'd arrive in time. He couldn't die – not Alasdair, the man who had seemingly defied death before, bouncing back even after breaking his spine in 2015, although confined to a wheelchair and without the use of his legs.

Yellow Pages

Our story began in 1981 when I was on the cusp of thirty, freshly separated from my husband and feeling rather lost. Lonely and emotionally frayed, I looked forward to a friend's party where Alasdair would also be a guest. Fast forward to today and I'm 73 and our friendship had weathered the test of time.

My first impression of him back then was a curious one. He struck me as friendly, albeit somewhat eccentric, though that night alcohol may have had a hand in his peculiar behaviour.

"Can I draw you?" he asked, seemingly out of the blue.

I couldn't find a reason to decline, and I must admit it was a flattering proposal.

Amidst a frantic search for a pencil and paper, our host handed him a pen and the back cover of the Yellow Pages, of all things. It was there that Alasdair Gray found May Hooper, in the Yellow Pages, of all places. Now, I understand that this reference might not resonate with the younger generation, accustomed to smartphones and social media, but trust me, it was an unconventional beginning.

"Do you still want to draw me?"

The sketch he created bore some resemblance to me, although it appeared somewhat genderless. I thanked him, and our host held on to the drawing.

"I'd like to draw you again, if that's okay," Alasdair declared.

"That would be nice," I replied.

But when I left the party that night we hadn't exchanged contact information.

Weeks later, almost forgetting that chance encounter, I found myself in the local pub with friends when I spotted him. He recognised me and flashed a grin that could have outshone a spotlight. With a smile of my own I couldn't resist asking, "So do you still want to draw me?"

"Oh, yes!" he practically shouted, drawing the bemused gaze of the pub's clientele. My face turned a bright shade of crimson.

And thus our lifelong friendship was born.

He gave me an address in the Hillhead area of Glasgow, on Kersland Street, and, when I knocked on his door, he greeted me with his characteristic grin that put me at ease instantly. His flat was massive, with several rooms sublet "to make ends meet". He explained that renting out rooms was the only way to afford the place, letting out a boisterous laugh in his signature stentorian, booming, Brian Blessed style. Many of his tenants, it seemed, weren't always prompt with the rent.

His personal room though was a study in contradiction. It was large, sparsely furnished and surprisingly tidy. There was a place for everything, and everything was in its place, which struck me as curious because Alasdair himself, with his mussed hair and mismatched clothing, wasn't particularly known for being neat. But I'll get to that later.

His peculiar approach to art was equally intriguing. Instead of the expected easel, he produced what I could only describe as a large board, material unknown. He unrolled a massive sheet of brown wrapping paper from a shelf, adding to my intrigue. I had to ask about the wrapping paper, and he explained that he preferred it over traditional canvases or other artist materials.

"It's very forgiving," he said, "and I've never been much good with skin tones. The buff background serves as a suitable skin shade."

I took his word for it, even though I had my doubts about everyone having buff skin.

I wasn't an artist; I was/am more of a doodler. Art materials and techniques weren't (at that time) my forte, but Alasdair's choices fascinated me. It turned out he had a fondness for Tippex as a medium, of all things.

He motioned for me to sit in a grand old-fashioned chair with rolled arms that I'll never forget. It was old, fabulous and, to be honest, a tad uncomfortable. The springs seemed to have a "personal vendetta against my bahookie", as he put it. Later, when the chair showed signs of wear, he had it re-upholstered, unwilling to part with it. I came to understand his attachment, as some of his finest works featured that very chair. There are paintings of me seated on it, but, interestingly, Alasdair, in his ever-contrary fashion, once decided to paint it out after completing a particularly exceptional work. In the finished piece it appeared as though I were floating in mid-air.

His reason? "I like the way it looks without the chair," he declared.

But let's return to that first sitting. I was now getting flustered, my cheeks flushed red, and I couldn't help but perspire.

"Don't be nervous," he reassured me. "It'll be fine."

He made it clear that sitting for him wasn't just about staying motionless.

"It's not all about keeping still," he explained.

And then, with a sudden urge for coffee, he offered, "Do you want a cup of coffee?"

Of course there was no milk. He cursed under his breath.

"One of these bloody buggers of flatmates of mine must've used the last of it!"

Well, perhaps his exact words weren't suitable for polite company, but you get the idea. It was a moment that had us both laughing uncontrollably, tears streaming down our faces.

I proposed that we venture out to Byres Road for some milk, not just for the coffee but to give us a chance to chat and get to know each other better before diving into the world of art. We grabbed our coats, and what was meant to be a quick milk run soon turned into a leisurely lunch at the local café, a two-hour conversation filled with stories from our pasts, from my abusive marriage and how I'd gone off the rails emotionally for a while to his ex-wife and the excitement surrounding his book, *Lanark*.

He agreed with my decision not to accept payment for modelling. I had no desire to become a professional model; I simply enjoyed his company.

"AND I GREATLY LIKE YOURS," he boomed, as was his way, drawing amused glances from the café crowd.

As he worked on his art, he had a curious habit of sticking out his tongue when deep in concentration – a quirk I found endearing, as it was one we shared.

A night at the Kelvingrove

Sometime after this, still in the early 1980s, I found myself at an exciting Midsummer Night's Ball, held at the splendid Glasgow Art Galleries, the Kelvingrove. There I was hand in hand with a male friend. The night promised enchantment, with laughter and dance swirling in the air – a sumptuous feast for all of my senses. As the evening wore on, a chance glance led me to spot my friend, Alasdair, dancing awkwardly, dad-dancing, with his companion. His eyes locked onto mine, and we exchanged smiles, adding to my overall good mood.

However, in the blink of an eye, the joyous atmosphere was shattered. Alasdair's girlfriend, who I didn't know at all at that time, fuelled by an inexplicable rage, surged towards me on the dance floor. With a swift and violent motion, she struck me hard in the face, and my teeth met my lips. Blood ran down, staining both my face and my dress in a grotesque display. She launched into a tirade, accusing me of encroaching upon her territory. Alasdair was her man!

"Leave him alone!"

I was stunned, speechless, threatened, not understanding a thing of what was happening.

Alasdair, seeing the assault, raced over, desperately pulling his incensed girlfriend away and imploring her to calm down. Disoriented and distressed, I turned to the chap I had been dancing with, saying I would need to go. I grabbed my coat and bag and ran. The night, once filled with joy, was now ruined, and I needed to tend to my injured face.

My partner wanted to stay. But I didn't. He advised me to call the police. I didn't want that.

I fled the Kelvingrove Gallery, turning onto Kelvin Way, Alasdair hot on my heels, his voice trembling as he repeated that she hadn't meant it, that it was all a terrible misunderstanding. It appeared he had also overheard whispers in the crowd, suggesting we call the police. My response to him was clear: she had acted deliberately. His pleas grew more frantic, he thought that I would change my mind about police involvement as there had been many witnesses. I walked briskly up University Avenue, assuring him that I was not going to involve the authorities. But I added, firmly, that I never wished to lay eyes on her again, her motive for the assault a baffling mystery to me.

Alasdair's eyes filled with tears, and he begged me to forgive her, explaining that she was plagued by jealousy. My heart, still pounding from the shock, remained resolute as I replied, "I don't think I ever will." It was then that he made a startling move. Overwhelmed with anguish, he dashed towards a lamppost, repeatedly striking his head against it until the blood flowed, a horrific sight that only added to my distress.

Rushing to his side, I saw the damage he'd inflicted upon himself. His forehead a landscape of swelling lumps, with blood streaming down his face, which dramatically and gruesomely underscored the bizarre turn this unforgettable evening had taken.

Considering his injuries and intoxicated state, I decided it would be best to go with him to his flat to tend to the cuts. Unfortunately, he only had micropore tape available, as opposed to steri-strips. I had a complete first aid kit at my place, but at that time, I lived some distance away on the south side of Glasgow.

I took him to his flat in Kersland Street and had a closer look at the damage to his face and head. Despite the swelling and bleeding, the cuts were superficial. However, I was concerned about a possible concussion. Alasdair, on the other hand, adamantly refused to let me call an ambulance or take him to the Western Infirmary's accident and emergency unit.

We were in quite a state, and I knew we'd both be dealing with bruises and swelling for several days – me with my sore face and bloody lip.

I decided to spend the night at his flat because of my concern about concussion. However there were no signs of that. I spent the night on a large chair, the chair he used in many paintings and also one I am depicted in. I tried to sleep but sleep was impossible. The next morning he awoke and appeared to be in pretty good shape. Initially he couldn't remember much about the night before. However after a couple of cups of tea his memory gradually returned and again he expressed deep embarrassment and regret for what had happened.

Did his hot-headed girlfriend come round to the Kersland Street flat? No, not while I was there. Did I hear from her again? Yes, she wrote me a letter of apology. I ripped it up. Alasdair also wrote me a letter apologising for his girlfriend's behaviour. I have stashed it away with the scores of other letters he wrote me.

I asked Alasdair why he felt he must punish himself physically for something his girlfriend did. He didn't answer. I don't think he knew.

I believed his self-destructive actions were concerning and I wondered if he had difficulties with confidence, with being candid – rather than tackle his frustration with others, he harmed himself physically? I, of course, did not say that out loud, I was quite reticent back then.

The morning after the ball, with Alasdair patched up and sobering up, I left Kersland Street and left him in his flat, my emotions all over the place, angry, upset, what the hell am I doing with these people, what are you doing May? I really don't get on with some of his crowd, I didn't understand them, so self-obsessed, but Alasdair you're different, I feel protective about you, you're putting your own life at risk by drinking so much and I can't just walk away from that. My head's a midden, my granny would have said your heid's full of wee broken bottles, you need to stop this now. This Alasdair's derailing me but what can I do, I can't NOT carry on seeing him. I just walked and walked around in the West End. I called my good friend Janet, my touchstone, and unloaded and she remembers the phonecall to this day.

I eventually went home and looked at my face in the mirror. Fecking hell!

After this Alasdair carried on seeing her for several more years. Had I known what sort of temper she had, I might never have agreed to model for Alasdair.

The borrowing of the radio

So at the time, I was living on the south side of Glasgow, on Paisley Road West. I didn't have a lot of money or possessions, but I had a radio. And I'd gone over to the West End to see Alasdair. He had asked me to come over. He had said he wanted to meet me because he wanted to draw me, to make a "nice painting" (those were his words). And I knew it would be fun. We always had a bit of a laugh and carry-on, and he had a good sense of humour and we got along well. But he was also going to tell me about something he had just done, something which he was regretting. What could this be?

Alasdair had a big flat, a rented third-floor flat on Kersland Street, a cavernous, cold, dilapidated tenement flat that he had acquired, some might say wangled, through a contact at the Glasgow City Council because, at the time, his first wife Inge and son Andrew were with him and justified the allocation of a council flat, albeit run-down, something that would not have been justified or allowed had a request come in from a single male penniless artist looking for a place to live and work and create. Alasdair sublet most of the rooms because he needed the money. There were a lot more than the average number of rooms that he let out to lodgers. He said he never got paid any rent too often but seemed to just accept that's how it was.

The flat was usually perishing cold and those who modelled for him had to suffer the cold. I remember the two-bar electric fire with its dangerous wiring. But for Alasdair space was more important than the fittings and the general condition of a place, although he himself kept all his stuff neatly arranged. He had a fear of confined spaces.

Then he told me about this event that was causing him such concern.

"I don't really know what to do, May, " he said. "I just don't know what to do. I was trying to concentrate on writing last night and all I could hear was a rrradio playing rrreally loud music. Blaring away. It was so loud I couldn't think, I couldn't hear myself think."

"That's terrible."

"So in the morning I just went through to the noisy bugger's room, took his rrradio and threw it out of the window. It crashed into smithereens on the pavement."

"Oh, you didn't do that? Oh my God!"

And he said, shaking, "And, and, when he came in, he asked me where his radio was. And it turned out that it wasn't him that had had the radio on, the sound was coming from another room, another lodger. And I threw out the wrong radio! I threw out the wrong one!"

And he was shouting and I was laughing. I couldn't stop laughing.

"Well, you'll have to apologise."

Alasdair said he had apologised.

I told him, "And you'll have to buy a new radio."

"But May, I can't afford it just now, can I borrow yours?"

"You can have my radio, I don't mind, just take it, I don't really use it very much."

"I'll take it, but it has to be our secret!"

"What do you mean?"

He explained, "Until I can afford to replace it because I've had to give him mine in the meantime."

I was puzzled. "Well, why does it have to be a secret? Just borrow mine or keep it, for God's sake!"

He said in his big loud voice, repeating himself anxiously, "Because, because if Bethsy knows you've given me a loan of your radio, YOUR RRRADIO, she will, she will be so angry with me! I can't can't can't let her know it's your rrradio."

So I had to keep it a secret for Alasdair's sake, even though I didn't see the point and thought it was silly. He was so afraid of his girlfriend finding out.

He actually came over to my flat soon after and took the radio away. I think he had it for about a month. When he returned it, I asked, "Did you manage to buy a new radio yet?"

"Yes, and I apologised again. I feel silly throwing the wrong radio out. But Bethsy still doesn't know I was using your radio myself and I need to give it back to you now."

"Alasdair, you can keep it for yourself."

But he insisted, "No, I can't because she'll know it's not my radio!"

Which I thought odd since she hadn't seemed to notice for weeks. He looked so scared, terrified even, of this person! He appeared genuinely frightened, which was at odds with him throwing out the wrong radio when he lost his temper. He didn't seem to know how to make up for that mistake, so was obviously more scared of his girlfriend than of the lodger. Did he have no nerves about confronting his lodger and explaining things to him yet he lived in trepidation of a confrontation with Bethsy? Alasdair and Bethsy never lived together, and I think she was very controlling, extremely controlling.

And what happened to the real radio culprit? I think word got around the flat that loud music late at night was inadvisable.

So here I was, battered in the face by a girlfriend of Alasdair's at the Midsummer Night's Ball and now experiencing the oddest effects that a supremely jealous woman had on my new friend's behaviour. What had I done? What was I guilty of? Apparently, as Alasdair told me in a letter, his girlfriend couldn't even bear the thought that he might be thinking about me. I had to believe him. So I was never allowed to say that he borrowed the radio from *me*. A long-held secret only now revealed.

Revelations

When I first met Alasdair, I was struggling to recover from the devastation inflicted by my abusive marriage. Years of physical and psychological torment had left me shattered, my trust in others fractured, and my will to live nearly extinguished. I unintentionally pushed away both those who wanted to stay and those I wanted to keep close.

Having experienced a relationship without genuine care and affection, I feared being mistreated again. This fear made it hard for me to allow others to get close, a realisation that only hit me years later. Loneliness and I suppose brokenness became constant companions, fuelling a cycle of self-isolation and despair – a pattern of unhealthy coping mechanisms.

I attempted to numb the pain by burying distressing memories and dismissing the lasting impact. These wounds persisted beneath an affectionate exterior, causing anxiety, hypersensitivity and a defensive tendency (particularly towards myself).

My abusive marriage left me with a profound sense of unworthiness, oscillating between complete isolation and a façade of gregariousness when with others. Despite attempting to forge new relationships after leaving my ex-husband, my distrust made genuine connections feel nearly impossible to attain.

Regardless, I found the strength to follow career aspirations and graduated as a nurse. Throughout my marriage, my ex-husband methodically shattered any optimism I had, intentionally sabotaging academic goals by tearing up my handwritten assignments. But once I got away, I worked hard to create a life of my own.

When I crossed paths with Alasdair I found a somewhat kindred spirit, someone who understood the weight of emotional hurt. We spent countless hours together, with him sketching and painting hundreds of pieces. He destroyed a lot but also kept many. I do not know where these are now. As I sat for him, we were able to engage in deeply revealing conversations. It was during these moments we shared experiences, delving into the depths of past traumas. For the first time, I opened up in graphic details and I thought recovering from the effects of abuse might become possible.

As our friendship deepened, spending hundreds of hours talking, shedding tears and sharing our vulnerabilities, I discovered that Alasdair's own marriage had left him feeling just as broken, despite the absence of physical abuse. These hours and hours of sharing intimate and often painful details created a closeness between us. Had we created a closeness that made Alasdair want more?

In spite of everything

Dear Alasdair,

I got your letter, and whilst I appreciate your honesty about your feelings towards me, I have to admit the explicit sexual nature of the content made me uneasy. While I appreciate your words and know that they are heartfelt, they didn't quite connect with me as you may have wanted. Rather than feeling moved, I felt disturbed.

I know how you feel about me, but I feel again I need to reiterate that I can't reciprocate those feelings in the way you want. Although our friendship is important to me, I think it's necessary to establish and respect boundaries, as I have mentioned before, especially given your relationship with your girlfriend.

It's unsettling to know that your girlfriend has negative emotions towards me, or as you mentioned, "hates me". I am not responsible for your feelings, and I hope we can address this and clarify the issue openly when we meet.

Although I've tried to understand and appreciate your optimism about me, I can't help but feel unsettled when it seems I am being discussed with another. I hope that my encouragement of your imaginations for stories hasn't fuelled these feelings.

There's more to discuss, but perhaps it's best saved for our meeting tomorrow. Can we please address these concerns openly and simply when we meet?
Love May X

Something Leather

The tale of *Something Leather* started life as a funny experience that I once had with Alasdair, something which eventually, after much laughter and chitter-chatter, developed into a story.

It was still the early 1980s, coming up to my birthday and at that time in my life, I generally wore only dresses or skirts with tops, mainly in the 30s or 40s style. I've been kind of hooked on that style forever. I didn't wear jeans then, although I do now. Back then I seldom wore trousers of any kind.

Alasdair and I had been out for a coffee and a drink (he had a drink and I had a coffee).

"I really want to buy you something for your birthday, May, something you would never think of for yourself."

"Thank you, that's really kind, but no, I don't need anything, I don't want anything."

I strongly suspected he would come up with a suggestion of something I wouldn't like, so had to be a little ungracious. There were things that he had been going on about for a while.

"You never wear trousers, that's not a complaint, you dress very well, but why no jeans?"

I told him my story about my ex-husband who didn't like me wearing trousers (and I didn't really mind that because I liked what I wore). But my ex was so controlling and abusive that I would've complied anyway – rather than get another black eye.

Alasdair was upset by that information (although he already knew about it) and insisted he buy me either a skirt or trousers that I'd never think of wearing, and to please let him choose. He was quite insistent, pleading almost.

I laughed. It was hysterical, because I wore lots of skirts.

"But this'll be something different, something leather," he said.

He mentioned leather trousers too, but I didn't fancy that idea at all, the thought of wearing such a garment and turning into a sweaty mess.

"No", he said. He'd buy both, the skirt and trousers. Again a firm no from me.

"So," said he, "at least let me get you a skirt, it'll just be something you can wear just once, for me – and maybe never want to wear it again."

I wasn't keen on the idea, but to keep him happy, because he never asked for much, I said OK, we'll get a leather skirt. And because I have particular tastes and didn't want to wear just any old skirt, I said that finding a nice one might be difficult. I didn't know if we could find what I would want to wear.

"Then we will just have some fun looking," said Alasdair.

We went to every leather shop in the centre of Glasgow and there weren't any skirts I liked. Thank goodness. And to be candid, I was pretty embarrassed. Every skirt he held up, I shook my head. I thought the skirts were trashy and horrid, but I began to get the idea about the way he wanted me to look.

In the last leather shop, when I shook my head again, he turned to the assistant.

"Can you rrrecommend any leather clothes makers, someone who will make a skirt or trousers to order?" he asked in his loud voice, as was his way.

"Yes, there's a place on the High Street," the woman replied.

She provided directions. The leather tailors were situated up a winding staircase in an old tenement building.

So we set off and I was getting anxious, unsure, and suggested we stop and think about this adventure. Alasdair got a little annoyed that I seemed to be changing my mind about all of this, so I suggested we go for a drink, somewhere near where we were then in the city centre.

But he wanted to keep heading east, on out towards the High Street, into a more run-down part of town. He saw a rough-looking pub – one of the most dangerous places you could imagine.

"Let's go in there," he said in his loud booming voice.

In he strode, me following reluctantly; the place was heaving with gangster types, real Glasgow hard men. This seemed to thrill him, but I was shaking, believing that at any minute a fight would break out and I would die, seeing how unusual we looked compared to the others in the bar. However that did not happen. We actually had a pretty jolly time and he downed two double whiskies and I had a soda. And during our time there I was persuaded about the leather skirt, I had lost the will to debate any further and I agreed to visit the little tailor's along the road on the High Street.

"This is where Glasgow started years and years ago, hundreds of years ago." Alasdair was keen to fill me in on some general local history. The tour guide in him came out.

We found the close number and climbed up an extremely well-worn stone staircase to the tailor's on the first landing. Old distemper peeling off the walls, the place was ancient. We rang the bell and a wee chunky woman came to the door. We went in. I was somewhat nervous. However the two women who ran the small establishment were delighted to see us.

Alasdair launched proceedings, (now remember he wasn't a controlling type – and I think he was feeling light-headed and happy because he was given this opportunity to be the one in charge).

"I would like to buy a leather skirt for my friend's birthday, and I wonder could you make it."

"Of course," the woman replied.

He had lots of ideas for a skirt: it should be very tight and short. But I did not like his ideas and said I would never wear anything like that. He relented.

"What *would* you wear?"

"Well, something maybe to my knees or past my knees, it would have to have big pockets so that I could stuff my hands into them when I get cold (I have cold hands). Probably an A line, something that I would be comfortable with, a waist that wasn't too tight, and perhaps a belt."

He agreed.

"It might also look nice with big buttons to do up the front," he suggested.

I replied that the buttons addition wasn't practical; but to make him happy I agreed on metal poppers, but they would have to be strong. Hearing our conversation, the women began laughing. One of them took out her measuring tape and began measuring my waist and hips and asked the length I wanted.

"Just past my knees please, perhaps to my calves."

So measurements were taken and I picked the softest leather imaginable and in black, although the black was Alasdair's choice. I would've preferred dark green. I'd never seen him look so happy.

Afterwards, seeing how his mood had changed and how ecstatic he was now, we went for something to eat and then home, each to our own. I was more than a little tired. And that should be where the story ended. But no.

We'd agreed to fetch the skirt from the tailor's within two weeks. However, when we returned, the door on the first landing no longer had the tailor's sign. It had closed. Alasdair was more upset than me. I really didn't mind that much. I simply accepted that it was not to be. However I'd forgotten that the woman had written down his name and address with the order. And he had paid in full.

We had no means of contacting the tailor. I left the close with a despondent Alasdair.

But two weeks later he called me in great excitement, telling me that the leather skirt had arrived in the post with an apology from the tailor and could I please come over to his place and try it on.

So I did as I was asked. I got the subway to Hillhead and went up to Kersland Street. When I rang the doorbell his face lit up and he couldn't wait for me to try it on. I didn't try it on in front of him. I went to the loo. It was a perfect fit.

"I can't wear this outfit outside, although it's decent. It makes me feel odd," I said.

"'I bet you can, just once to please me?"

Given that it was a perfectly respectable skirt, ending below my knees, I agreed to wear it once. Although it just wasn't me. Anyway, within a couple of weeks he arranged a pub outing where I would wear the skirt. This delighted him.

I wore it with a thin silk blouse and short black leather boots. He was thrilled. I got some odd looks because folks who knew me also knew I'd never dress that way. I only wore it once. He also asked to draw me wearing it. It wasn't a huge request, so I agreed, I actually expected him to ask. That drawing graces the cover of some of his books and it's hidden away somewhere now, I can't remember where. I still have the skirt – and the boots and the original manuscript of *Something Leather*.

Bowling

We got on a train, got off at Bowling and began one of our walks. Or tramps as he liked to call them. The sky was totally and unbrokenly blue as only a Scottish sky can be. Alasdair was ecstatic. Jubilant. I didn't know where we were going, but I trusted him. Out in the country he was a fast walker. In town he was more of a shuffler. Alasdair found a path. I have since discovered that the path was an old railway line. There were trees to my left and a path on the right with fields in the distance, at least that's how I remember it. My sense of direction was laughably bad then, and I had problems finding my way out of a paper bag. I didn't know where he had taken me. I could see water somewhere off in the distance.

"What's that over there?" says I, pointing to the water.

"That's the Firth of Clyde."

As we walked, he started telling me about some negative reviews he'd got about *1982, Janine*. He was a wee bit upset but wouldn't admit it.

I remember the walk took place sometime after our wee jaunt into Glasgow city centre in search of something leather for my birthday. He suggested we could counter the Janine sexist critiques by writing something from a strong female perspective. He wanted me to think about it.

I suggested it would be a good idea if he wrote about the day we'd bought the leather skirt, developing it as a short story and perhaps that would inspire him. (But I wasn't sure that writers needed inspiration; wasn't it just a case of planking your arse on a seat and beginning to see where your head took you?)

Alasdair said he thought it a better idea if it was me who developed the events of that day as a short story and, if I was up for it, a book. And he suggested that while I was writing it, he would pretend to be my creative writing tutor and I should pretend to be his student and he would supervise me to make sure I was on track. He became excited by the idea. The notion of role-play thrilled him; he would be in charge of me through my work. He would bloody love that. I laughed, and he joined in, although he had no clue what I was laughing about.

I said that I couldn't do justice to such a book, and although it was me who'd suggested a short story, I also didn't believe there was enough material from the trip to town to compose an entire book.

"OK, I'll need to think about it."

"YES, YOU CAN DO IT MAY if you put your mind to it!"

He was quite sharp when he said this and I felt reprimanded, but it was nice that he had more faith in me than I did. I knew he was complimenting me, but I had an idea about what he would want me to write and I wasn't at a stage of my life where I was comfortable with the development of the not-so-subtle sex scenes he'd want. (Alasdair often had fantasies involving lesbian relationships.) I think I could do it now, but don't want to.

He even wrote me a letter where he again proposed that I write the story and he would be there pretending to be my creative writing tutor. Maybe he wrote the letter having forgotten our discussion. He was, after all, consuming whisky from a flask on that walk, well on all our walks, to be frank.

Alasdair and I had become very close and, knowing that I lacked the confidence to write about our leather adventure, he said he would write a wee book about me. His plan was also to include every depiction ever painted or sketched (and there were scores of them) with some stories of our times together. It was to be called *The Book of May*. However, life's busyness interfered, and the project never materialised.

A hospital visit

It was the autumn of 1985 and I had recently moved into my new flat on Marchmont Terrace. It took some time to get the place habitable: the last owners had cut off all the lighting wires so that they were left flush with the ceiling, some of the floorboards were rotten and there was a big tarpaulin covering the missing parts of the roof. Nice. But it wasn't a slum, just an old and neglected place. And I was happy with it. The Terrace is quite high up at the summit of the hill going up from Byres Road and there is a steep little curving bit of pavement just before you reach the level of the Terrace. Walking out one late autumn evening I slipped on some wet leaves, fell over backwards and cracked my head on the pavement.

They admitted me to the now-demolished Western Infirmary. I don't remember much about how I got from the slippery pavement to A&E, but I do remember the events that followed. I think initially there may have been a question about a concussion. They'd found a hairline fracture.

Now the thing was, at that time I was working as a staff nurse in that same hospital and, although I was in a single side room, it was highly embarrassing when the ward round was happening because who should come around but doctors and a nurse that I knew. Medical people always found it hilarious when one of their own was admitted. Anyway the examination took place. Although I was recovering well, they wanted me to stay as an in-patient for several days for observation. Had to be. My mood was unsurprisingly low.

A doctor I knew made a joke.

"What are you like, May! I think we'll pin your skull X-ray up on the canteen wall so that everyone will think you fell over when you were drunk."

"What?"

"Of course I'm kidding, May, you know that."

But everyone there took the joke as intended; he was trying to cheer me up; and it worked. We all laughed out loud. And I immediately felt better.

Later that day when visiting time came round, in rushed my mother, looking worried.

"May, for heaven's sake, what's happened to you?"

"Hello Mum. I slipped and cracked my skull."

"Had you been to the pub, May?"

"Mum, I never drink before going on shift, you know that."

"Well, you need to watch where you're putting your feet."

Anyway she hugged me. A hug from Mum was a rarity.

I felt I had to explain how I tripped and fell. I took a deep breath.

"Mum, the pavement was all slippery wet with leaves. I didn't notice them in the dark. You know I wasn't at the pub, I wouldn't have done that. And the medical staff here know that too, it would have been recorded when I was admitted if I had alcohol in me. And I didn't have any alcohol in me."

"Well, thank goodness for that."

As my Mum was sitting there, getting only slightly re-assured about the reason for my mishap, suddenly from down the corridor a loud booming voice interrupted us, a bit of a relief as it broke the unwelcome tension of being wrongly accused of an accident beyond my control. The voice was coming towards my room, get-ting closer and louder. The voice belonged to Alasdair, who was pleased to see me, as he was also loudly let-ting everyone in the hospital know. There was a woman with him. She looked pleasant, but I had never met her before, and I wasn't sure if this was a new girlfriend or just a friend. My mum looked at them, alarmed. Oh God, what now!

I knew my mother could be judgmental. Alasdair was his usual rather shabbily dressed self and his friend seemed nice, but both of them were a wee bit the worse for wear, Alasdair considerably more so. I introduced them to my mother. Alasdair spoke.

"Hello, May, can I introduce you to Agnes." He stopped before going further. "Ah? So you're May's mother? Pleased to meet you." He held out his hand and my Mum looked even more startled. But she did shake his hand.

"And this is Agnes Owens. Agnes is also a writer." Agnes shook hands with us.

Mum awkwardly said hello. I knew by the shocked look on her face that she didn't approve. I knew she was wondering how on earth I knew these people. I thought both of them were delightful and they'd made the effort to physically visit to cheer me up. This was the first time Alasdair visited me in the hospital (although it wasn't to be the last).

I don't know how Alasdair knew I was in hospital. This was all before mobile phones; however we know there are jungle drums out there, so someone must've let him know. They stayed a while, regaling me with stories about what was happening and we had a good laugh. But I could see Mum getting more and more uncomfortable.

After about 20 minutes Agnes and Alasdair got to their feet and left. They had somewhere to go. Alasdair and I weren't neighbours then; we were close friends. I lived on

Marchmont Terrace and Alasdair was still on Kersland Street. He didn't move to the Terrace until 1991.

When the two of them had left my little room, Mum's face was a study.

"May. Honestly, I don't know. What sort of friends have you got? What company are you keeping? How do you know this jakey? So that's the man who did that portrait of you."

True. I had given my Mum a portrait that Alasdair had done of me, had had it framed specially for her.

"Calls himself an artist! Huh! That picture he did of you! Terrible, so it is! Terrible. It doesn't look a bit like you. He makes you look ugly. That's not my beautiful daughter."

Mum was clearly more than a little upset by Alasdair's picture of me that I had given her as a present. In fact she gave it back to me.

"I'm not having that hanging on a wall in my house! And he dresses like a tramp."

I was a touch angry with Mum for saying things like that. Alasdair's clothes were perhaps mismatched, but he wasn't dirty. He had good personal hygiene. Mum often judged people by appearances. But then so did most people and there would often be odd looks when Alasdair and I were out together. On certain occasions Alasdair would dress up in a nice white shirt, the Liberty braces

that I bought him, a wool pullover and dark blue cor-
duroy trousers, especially when going out to eat. The
sandals added to the 50s hippie look.

I was discharged a short time afterwards and went back
to work at the Western and they were pleased to have me
back. Always short-staffed. Nothing has changed.

Nights at the pictures

Alasdair loved going to the pictures (and when he could he would buy the tickets). We often went to the cinema together, just the two of us, sometimes in town to the Odeon, the GFT or wherever they were playing something we wanted to see. We also saw films at the Salon and the Grosvenor in the West End. Sadly, the Salon no longer exists, but the Grosvenor although closed for a while has reopened. It was always Alasdair who would invite me out to the cinema, ringing me up or coming round to my flat. And we would go for a couple of drinks first, the usual double whisky for Alasdair and a glass of white wine for me. And it was always just the two of us: Bethsy wouldn't go with him and later on Morag wasn't interested in the cinema.

Thanks for your letter Alasdair. Glad to hear that Bethsy is now ok with you going to the cinema with me. But can I really believe it? No, I can't. Why should I be concerned about something like that? But I must say that didn't worry me in the slightest, although I

was generally a bit concerned about her reactions.
When's the next film? I do so love going to the pictures
with you.
Love May

We had several cinematic adventures. But there are a
handful of films that made him feel excited and remain
etched in my memory.

One vivid recollection dates back to the mid-1980s, a
time when Alasdair and I went to see a film – and the
experience is unforgettable – *Back to the Future*, featur-
ing Michael J. Fox and Christopher Lloyd. As the lights
dimmed, Alasdair became visibly animated and I could
feel his excitement, kind of like heat spreading from his
body, fidgeting in his seat like a wee boy. In fact going to
the pictures with Alasdair was always like taking a little
boy on a special outing. He took such a childlike delight
in the films.

Much of his cheerfulness was directed at Doc Brown
in the film and his unruly head of hair – maybe it was
because Alasdair too was constantly behaving similarly,
running his fingers through his hair, making it a tad wild
– identifying with Doc Brown?

He loved the name of Doc's invention, the 'flux capac-
itor', which could allow the time machine to either go
back in time or forward into the future. Alasdair muttered

something about HG Wells, but I really couldn't make out quite what he was saying and certainly didn't want to start up a conversation let alone a discussion. I was trying to concentrate on the film for heaven's sake, and I thought the audience was getting annoyed as I could hear tutting.

"Alasdair, shhh, please."

He quietened down for a bit. But it wouldn't last. He really had no awareness that his reactions and outbursts could be a problem for other people.

When he saw the time machine in the form of a converted DeLorean, which I believe the Doc fuelled with plutonium, Alasdair just couldn't contain himself. He let out a loud whoop and, to the amusement of the audience, sprang to his feet, although some eyebrows were raised. I only felt a slight twinge of embarrassment, being used to his somewhat outlandish behaviour. But of course there was always the fear at the back of my mind that we would be asked to leave, if we couldn't be quiet.

I stupidly tried to ground his enthusiasm and explained that the DeLorean was an actual car, a real car that actually existed. However, Alasdair, unfamiliar with the model, dismissed this revelation as if it did not matter. He thought it was a fantasy car. But to be candid, this only added to his charm.

In the film when Marty travels back to the 1950s it is Marty rather than George, his present-day father, who is hit by Lorraine's father's car and is cared for in the family home. Lorraine, his present-day mother, is taking care of him. It is a slightly uncomfortable scene for the audience because we know that she is his present-day mother and that she fancies him. But Alasdair loved this. He found it titillating. I wasn't sure if it was about potential incest or not, but the audience's mood quickly lightened when Lorraine insisted on calling Marty 'Calvin'. When Marty asked why, she replied that it was because "it says so on your underwear" and she said that she had never seen purple underwear before. This scene prompted hoots of laughter from the audience.

"Why are they laughing?" asked Alasdair.

Alasdair turned to me, puzzled, seeking an explanation for the laughter. In the lowest whisper I could manage I clarified that Marty's underwear had the designer label 'Calvin Klein', and back in the 1950s the concept of label snobbery was unknown, so the audience's amusement was at seeing the designer's name on the underpants instead of the wearer's own name. Alasdair, delighted by this titbit, couldn't fathom why designers would put personal insignia on underwear. And he had never heard of Calvin Klein. There were clear limits to his areas of interest or awareness. This time it was me who laughed out loud. But this only added to an already grand night at the pictures.

Back to the Future is actually one of the funniest memories I have of our times at the pictures.

We also went to see *Raiders of the Lost Ark* and Alasdair again got into thon wriggly excited way. The hero Indiana Jones gets up to all sorts of impossible stuff. When a huge boulder comes rolling down and chases Indy in a cave, Alasdair jumped up out of his seat, whooping with excitement, almost giving me a heart attack. Other members of the audience were equally excited but didn't show it in quite the same way.

Many years later, after his accident, when he could no longer walk, we would watch films together in his home on Marchmont Terrace. I would take my iPad down and we would sit there and watch. We would sometimes watch art films – and during these he would be silent, concentrating on the film.

Walks on the Necropolis

Many of our walks took place on the Glasgow Necropolis, the Victorian cemetery on a hill just behind the cathedral and the Royal Infirmary. It came into existence in 1833 and Alasdair saw it as Glasgow's Père Lachaise, the grand Parisian cemetery.

Regardless of how frequently we visited, Alasdair always found excitement there in its remarkable architecture and sculptures, sharing fascinating stories during these times.

He often pointed out the monument to John Knox, using it as a launching pad for intriguing Knox information. Initially, my interest lay more in the simple pleasure of walking and reading tombstones. However, Alasdair's enthusiasm compelled me to delve deeper and expand my knowledge about the cemetery's history and the people buried there.

He told me that there were over 3,000 tombs on the Necropolis, although he mercifully spared me from a meticulous tomb count. Alasdair also pointed out monuments and memorials in prominent locations, such as the one commemorating William Miller, a cabinetmaker from Dennistoun, the Glasgow district just a little further east. Unfamiliar with Miller, I was taken aback when Alasdair revealed Miller was the poet behind *Wee Willie Winkie*, a poem deeply ingrained in Scottish childhood (and known much further afield as well). I knew it well. Sadly, Miller died destitute.

It is clear that Alasdair would have made an excellent Glasgow tour guide, although his propensity to become over-excited would probably have resulted in him being fired.

During one of our walks, I could feel Alasdair getting a little nervy. This wasn't unusual, he started stuttering a bit, I just knew he was on the point of saying something which he wasn't sure I would like. Out it came.

"Do you think, do you think you could ever live with me? Or we could get married. We're such good friends and you're like me and we get on really well."

"What do you mean I'm like you?"

"Well, for one thing, we both go off at tangents."

"True."

"For God's sake Alasdair, do you make a habit of proposing to women in cemeteries?"

He laughed out loud.

"See what I mean? Snappy phrases, we could make a good couple."

"That'll be shining bright!" I said. "You know I adore you, but I don't love you in that way. But I do love you."

We carried on walking, Alasdair not put out. Well, not much. I thought this conversation would come up again. And it did.

He really believed that our strong friendship could handle such a bond, even though I wasn't physically attracted to him. I responded, expressing my belief that our bond would endure longer if we remained friends and might not last if we changed the relationship.

"I just had to ask," he said.

Unsurprisingly, he revisited the question on another walk, undeterred by my initial response.

Eventually, Alasdair understood and, in a letter which I received shortly after this, acknowledged that maintaining our friendship was likely the best course. This told me that he had given some thought to this arrangement, understanding that remaining friends was for the best.

He said I gave him energy and inspired him, that he believed he knew himself better through knowing me. When discussing books, he said that it was essential for us to play with fire and not be consumed by it, because he thought that my heart was warmer than his and although he'd cope, perhaps I wouldn't. I don't know if this was to make him feel better about the friendship issue, but if it helped, it was no bad thing. Life and art, the two intertwined.

Ultimately, he said that he thought my only allowing him the nearness of sketching me was good for him – because drawing was not a substitute for simple sex, it could be much more. The drawings were made to show me, more or less, offering myself to the world and if we were together or married, he wouldn't want to give me away like that. He always said that ours would remain the queerest kind of intimacy. These were his words. He had an odd way of speaking sometimes.

And although I could never fulfil the role of lover he initially desired, I remained the woman who loved him as a friend unconditionally.

Dear Alasdair,

I'm writing to you about our recent conversation about marriage during our walk the other day. Upon reflection, I realise that my response may have come across as flippant or awkward, and I want to provide a more thoughtful explanation. When I said, "I don't love you in that way", it didn't fully convey my true feelings.

Alasdair, you mean the world to me. Our friendship is one of the most important and cherished relationships of my life. However, as much as I adore you, my feelings for you are not sexual in nature. This is not a reflection on you but simply a matter of where my heart leads me.

Please know that I did not dismiss your proposal lightly. I thought about it very seriously. Ultimately, I cannot commit to a marriage when I don't have those sexual feelings you want. I fear it would risk irreparable harm to our incredible friendship, which I value deeply.

You also said that our friendship would endure longer than any marriage, and I wholeheartedly agree, but I was afraid that I had hurt you, so thank you for these words which helped ease my feelings of guilt.

What we share is profoundly special precisely because it exists outside the bounds of a traditional couple relationship, transcending conventional labels which I believe will endure the tests of time.

I hope you can understand. My love and care for you go beyond what words can express, but not in the conjugal sense you hoped for. Please know this decision does not diminish how vital you are to me. I simply cannot be your wife, as much as I wish I could make it so for your sake.

Love May X

The Edinburgh Book Festival

The year was 1985, and Alasdair and I went through to the Edinburgh Book Festival together. Alasdair was to give a reading, and it was all very bewildering to me. I felt like a fish out of water because there were all these literary types and lots of authors there and I didn't see myself as being a literary type and certainly not an author. I felt quite intimidated.

Jimmy Boyle's book *A Sense of Freedom* had just been republished and I actually got to speak to him together with Alasdair. At that point in the proceedings I was not so much intimidated as scared stiff, although Alasdair chatted away quite happily with him.

As the day progressed and after he did his wee bit, there was lots of drinking, and Alasdair got really, really, really drunk.

When I was out with Alasdair, I didn't drink very much because I knew one of us had to be compos mentis and if you had ever tried to stop Alasdair from drinking, you would know what I'm speaking about.

So when the time came to get the train home to Glasgow, I assisted him in staggering on board; the train was packed full of people returning from Edinburgh to Glasgow. I was a bit embarrassed – read very – in charge of this seriously drunk man.

Alasdair was in a state of excitement after such a fascinating day. His face was flushed crimson, and I was worried. We found a seat. But he closed his eyes and quickly fell asleep and a more or less normal complexion returned, and this made me happy. I didn't enjoy seeing him in such a high state of excitement, afraid he might have a stroke or some other cardiovascular event. His head lolled onto my lap, dribbling, drooling. My skirt got wetter and wetter and ended up soaking wet.

People opposite were looking over and laughing, and I didn't know what to do, so I did nothing but gently smile back while raising my eyebrows and widening my eyes in a kind of caring but "what can you do" sort of way. But I was actually GLAD he was asleep and comfy on my lap.

Although I was embarrassed by the spectacle we presented, his sleeping state caused me relief, despite my discomfort. His state of unconsciousness shielded me from what could have become "intoxicated storytelling", which might have alienated our fellow travellers.

His (frequent) descent into drunken ramblings or musical interludes was entertaining, and I loved that in him, but I didn't know if the passengers would have appreciated it. And I didn't know if he'd be in singsong or orator mode. I just couldn't know, but I DID know that I wouldn't be able to manage such a performance, so I let him slumber and gladly endured the amused glances, grateful for his calm.

He slept until we got to Glasgow. And I had to shake him awake, otherwise we wouldn't have got off the train. We got a taxi home. He went back to his enormous flat on Kersland Street and me to my flat in Marchmont Terrace, where I'd not long moved in.

People ask why I put up with this. The explanation for why I put up with this is quite simple, in case you're wondering. I saw a lot in him and I also learned a lot from him. He was a mine of information, especially in the fields of local history and the history of socialism. And he was generally great fun to be with.

I often thought of him as a very clever little boy, a savant if you like, afraid to grow up. There was an innocence to him, so when attempting adult mode – and wanting to orate in full flow, he'd indulge in drink – well, at least that was my impression.

He could talk for hours about world affairs, his knowledge was enormous, and his assessment skills of why he believed awful stuff happened were excellent.

He would speak for hours about the cause of poverty, the cruelties of the oppression of the poor and how those in power knew how keeping folks poor could serve their purpose. As he told the stories, his anger would grow, and his voice became shriller. He delivered his speeches with fervour and passion. I appreciated the depth of empathy and insight that he revealed to me.

While it is true Alasdair's knowledge was extensive, his grasp of contemporary issues appeared (to me) somewhat arrested. When discussing a notable news story, he would often say, "Thank you, I did not know that" and I'd be stunned when he told me he was also learning from me. And that pleased me enormously.

A bit of the West Highland Way

Alasdair and I would often go for long walks. He loved it. When you're walking, you're talking and we talked about everything and anything, some things interesting, some funny, some frivolous and some quite philosophical. On these walks we discussed ideas. We could let our imaginations run.

He remarked that some of the things I said gave him ideas. When he said he found my musings interesting I usually laughed, but it also delighted me. Nonetheless it was Alasdair that usually occupied most of the talking space, he could talk non-stop (he was a fabulous story-teller). But he listened when I spoke. We'd become confidants.

Alasdair was asthmatic and always had an inhaler in his pocket, but on our walks he never needed to use it. He was a changed person in the open air.

He would also talk about people who were important in his life, in particular he would talk about writers and artists that he had been friends with. Way back in the 1950s he had been great friends with a painter called Alan Fletcher whom he met at Glasgow School of Art. He would talk about Alan Fletcher more than anyone else. Alasdair had been very impressed by Alan's abilities and was more than slightly jealous of Alan's attractiveness to women. The way he talked about Alan made me think that Alasdair had some sort of male crush on Alan Fletcher, the way he described his good looks and long flowing dark hair and devilish charming smile. It was in 1958, when in Italy, that Alan went over a wall and fell to his death.

One day in the mid-1980s we decided it would be good to walk part of the West Highland Way. Neither of us were too fit, so we got a train to Milngavie where the West Highland Way begins. Alasdair was seeing his jealous Bethsy at this time and we had to keep our walks a secret from her or else she would have forbidden him to go with me.

It wasn't a great day weather-wise but it wasn't too cold, and the sun shone intermittently. We trudged through Mugdock Park into an area where there is a building known as Khyber Cottage; I don't even know if it's still there. And then when we arrived at Craigallian Loch it began raining, not too heavy, but smirry, as we say in Scotland. Just a wee smirr. I remember we were near a burn, a tributary of the Allander Burn. The ground had flooded, making it muddy and puddly and the mud clung tightly to our shoes; it didn't help that Alasdair's shoes were leather slip-ons.

Alasdair's customary country rain hat

We came to a country stile. I wanted him to go over first, worried that he would fall as his shoes had no grip. I worried about him a lot. I saw Alasdair was vulnerable, that much of his loud voice and his wish to be heard was often really a performance. He was never show-offy when it was just us.

He started the climbing manoeuvre. He put one foot on the ground by the stile and the other onto the stile itself. And that foot which he put on the ground landed

73

in a particularly muddy patch. The area near the stile had been filling with water and his foot was stuck fast in the mud and he couldn't pull it out. Alasdair got off the stile like a ballerina, twirling his unstuck leg and almost losing his balance as the other foot remained stuck in the mud. He held on to me and I held on to the stile for safety and after a huge heave the ground released his foot. But all we removed from the boggy ground was a wet foot and a soggy sock. The shoe was lost.

Upset and becoming angry, mainly with himself for wearing "stupid stupid shoes" and for not paying attention to the muddy ground.

He kind of lost his temper, but not quite. He put his hand into the muddy pool and swirled it around trying to locate the shoe and simultaneously soaking the cuff of his jacket, but he couldn't find it.

He supposed it had disappeared for good into the mud. "Like quicksand," he muttered, annoyed with himself. His reaction didn't surprise me as Alasdair could exhibit a child-like quality that I sometimes found endearing, and his reaction to losing the shoe was one of a toddler tantrum and I had to steel myself from laughing – that would just have made things worse.

"Just leave the damned shoe, leave it, leave it, leave it! I don't need it, let's go, I'll manage with the one!" he spluttered.

Stuck in the mud

"Don't be daft, we can't do that; there's a long way to go – there's no shop for miles. You need both shoes. Calm down, go stand over there for a minute and I'll see if I can get it."

And I pointed to a dry patch of ground.

I was getting irritated, and I hated that feeling, so I took a deep breath and smiled at him as he moved on to the dry patch and that seemed to help ease his distress – and mine.

I peered into the muddy puddle and thought, this is going to be deep. Taking off my jacket and jumper, I stuck my hand into the muddy water, and it was deep, really deep. I couldn't find the shoe; I then rolled up the short sleeve of my T-shirt, stuck my arm into the puddle and went deeper, my other hand holding on to the wooden post of the stile. The mud gurgled past my elbow almost up to my armpit and then I felt more solid earth and touched the shoe. My arm became coated in black mud, but I had the shoe.

I breathed a sigh of relief, and he looked over at me with a slightly mortified look on his face. What could I say? I told him that I wished I'd brought my camera.

"Ach that's a shame. We could've got great pictures." And that helped put the incident in perspective, we weren't dead or injured after all, just mud-covered dafties.

There were some snacks wrapped in a towel inside my backpack and I used the towel to wipe my arm and then I put on my jumper. I was shivering. I dried the badly behaved shoe as best I could with the now dirty towel. He had already removed his sock; it was wringing wet and I slipped on the shoe a tad Cinderella-like, although I didn't feel at all like Prince Charming.

The leather was slippery, but it was better than walking with bare feet, I thought – I was so wrong! Before we had gone 100 yards, I saw he was wobbling, his foot was sliding around in the slithery shoe, and I feared he would fall.

But the sun was coming out and warming the air and, I should add, also me after my muddy plunge. I suggested we stop and sit in the warmth for a little while to figure things out. I dried his sock as best I could, wrapping it in the (by now black) towel and squeezing out the water, stretching it over a rock to dry as we sat and chatted for about half an hour. That was easy. Alasdair loved to talk.

We were getting cold, so I had a feel of the sock, which although still damp would be wearable for a wee while.

"Well damp sock is better than no sock and breaking your leg. At least you'll be able to walk."

Alasdair found this funny and put the damp sock on. And on we trudged.

But there was one thing I just had to bring up.

"Alasdair, about that letter you sent me the other day, one of your unwise ones."

"Mmm?"

"You really can be a dirty old bugger, Mr Gray. I suppose you'd've had a few drinks before you wrote it. But then you usually have had a few drinks."

"Ha. Quite right."

"Anyhow the answer is still no. No I won't and no you can't."

"Ah. Thought you'd say that."

"I wonder sometimes… Mind that cowpat! …are you just rehearsing a theme or a passage from a new novel you're working on?"

"Mmm, well…"

"I mean so is this really a kind of fiction that you're sending me?"

"Well, in a way it…"

"Or is it fiction which you're hoping to turn into reality?"

"Yes, well…"

"Because I want you to know that I'm keeping these letters, because I do value them just as much as I value our unusual friendship."

"So you don't want me to stop writing then?"

"I do and I don't. Maybe someday someone will research it all and write whole screeds about the artistic imagination and what a life you lead inside your head and how that sparks the literary process."

"Ha. God help us all."

"Quick, here's the bus coming."

The Jolly Boys

A huddle of men around some pub tables pushed together, bottles of beer and glasses of wine and whisky on each table. A lot of laughter and a growing sense of anticipation.

"We're getting cannons tonight."

"And the valley of Death."

"You sure he's coming?"

"Aye, but who knows…"

"I reckon he'll be along. He won't be missing this. Not that old bugger."

"Cannons to the right of them. Cannons to the left of them."

"There's no 'the' in it. You've got it wrong."

"It wouldnae work without the 'the.'"

"Aye, it would too. It's fine like that."

"Well, you'll have to get Alasdair to sort it out."

"He's the Paul McCartney of Scottish culture and literature! That's what he is!"

They all laughed at the absurd comparison. But it showed the respect they held him in. A deep respect. This was a Jolly Boys event, a men-only session of like-minded whisky drinkers.

"And did you hear he's just turned down a knighthood?"

"Eh? You're kidding."

"He wouldnae know where to put it."

"And a couple of honorary doctorates too."

"Arise Sir Alasdair." Loud laughter and puzzled looks.

The pub door opened a crack and was then flung back and in came the Bard of Byres Road, welcomed by cheers from the Jolly Boys in the huddle around the table.

"Alasdair! Good to see you, man! In you come! Get the man a chair!"

"Have a dram."

"First of the evening, eh? Bet you've just about forgotten what it tastes like."

Raucous laughter filled the space the Jolly Boys had hired for the evening in the pub.

Alasdair had first met George Tomlinson, the main organiser of the Jolly Boys, decades before, way back in the early 60s when they were both taking part in a Polaris demonstration in Glasgow. They became friends, George and Alasdair. And the Jolly Boys groups found him top-quality entertainment and enjoyed his company and then around 1981, when *Lanark* had just come out, they all realised what a proposition they had here. And they held him in "exceptionally high esteem". Those words were carefully chosen and sincere and totally without the slightest trace of sarcasm.

And when Alasdair got excited, which he always did, he could go into a frenzy of speaking and reciting, and they loved that. They absolutely loved that. It wasn't long before:

"Half a league, half a league,

Half a league onward,

All in the valley of Death

Rode the six hundred."

Great cheers and intent listening from all the Jolly Boys, all at the same time.

"Have another, Alasdair."

"Don't mind if I do."

"Cannon to right of them,

Cannon to left of them,"

"See, nae 'the'."

"When can their glory fade?"

They loved that line. It chased around the corners of the pub room.

Alasdair's performance reached a huge climax. Wild applause. What else. *The Charge of the Light Brigade* was the all-time favourite.

George reminded them all of the time they had all gone to a Burns Supper in the Provand's Lordship, quite a formal event. Well, usually. And Alasdair used to tie his trousers up with a piece of cotton or some string. Anyway, Alasdair got quite drunk and when he stood up his trousers fell down.

"That was before his friend, May Hooper, bought him a pair of Liberty braces."

"Here's to May and the Liberty braces!"

"Aye, cheers!"

Of course, I was never allowed to be there at these men-only events. I'd hear about it all afterwards, well the bits that they could remember. And the Jolly Boys met up year after year and Alasdair would go along just as often as he possibly could.

May 1988

Dear Alasdair

Thank you so much for your letter telling me what has happened with Something Leather. *I know you really wanted me to write that story, but I just couldn't, really couldn't, although you were giving me lots of help and pretending to be a writing course teacher. And it's probably a good thing that I didn't write it, since you have had such a great success with it in the way that you did it. And to hear that you got a really good advance from the publisher is just brilliant. A whole novel, that's unbelievable! Can't wait to read it. See what happens when you buy me a birthday present like that leather skirt! Magic powers, eh? But honestly it's not me that made you rich, as you claim. You did that. Well maybe I helped a wee bit. I'll never forget that time when we went out together looking for a tailor who could make leather things. It was such fun, but more than just a little scary for me, with you taking me to parts of Glasgow where I'd never been before and wouldn't ever have dreamt of going to. All those scary-looking characters who were actually really friendly when you got talking to them. Yes, do get in touch again when you want to draw me again. I'm honestly not sure what to reply to you talking about us never having made love. Maybe if we had, I wouldn't have made you rich. There's a thought for you.*

Anyway here's a big hug from your good friend

May

PART TWO

20 Park Circus

I had contacted a friend of mine on Alasdair's behalf because Alasdair wanted to send a piece of writing to a publisher in New York.

"I know someone who has one of those new-fangled fax machines. He could probably help you there. He's got an office in Park Circus."

"Well, that could be part of our next walk in Kelvingrove Park. What do you say?"

So one fine day soon after, off we went, Alasdair and I, on a tramp to Kelvingrove Park, him with his papers in his rucksack. As always our talk was non-stop and fairly wide-ranging.

"So are you still thinking of chucking nursing, May? Is it not the thing you want to be doing any more?"

"I am, yes."

"We need nurses. I know we depend on doctors, but nurses would be all we need if we all improved our diets. Nutrition! Nutrition is at the bottom of everything."

"But your diet is terrible!"

"You can't expect me to practise what I preach."

We had a good laugh.

"I'd like to become a medical social worker. I see people coming into hospital and being discharged without the cause of their problem being addressed. How can I do something about that?"

"Treating the symptoms and not the cause, you mean. You're quite right. But what can we do? I take it you mean social causes and not physiological causes."

We walked on.

"Let's go over to the steps. Past the Stewart Memorial. His office is not far from the top."

"Look at the state of that memorial! Terrible! How can the Council neglect it like that!" Alasdair launched off into a history of the Stewart Memorial. He was so maddened by the way it had been let go.

We got to the steps. Alasdair fairly leapt up them, leg problems (he had leg ulcers) not showing at all. I followed at a more leisurely pace.

"It's number 20. Next door but one to where Godwin and Bella Baxter live at number 18. What a coincidence!" But they weren't at home.

Alasdair stood looking up at the building. Took a deep breath and went in.

A few days later my friend told me how a quite subdued and quiet Alasdair had come up the stairs to his office with his sheet of foolscap paper written in longhand on both sides and from one edge to the other, no margin left at all. The others in the office had been quite excited to see a famous author coming in. One of them put the paper in the fax and dialled the New York number. Alasdair watched nervously as the paper started to disappear with a light grinding noise into the body of the machine. He didn't have a copy. Alasdair never had copies. Oh God, what's happening? Where's my document going?

"Never fear, it's all in hand," said the girl.

Then the paper emerged unscathed, and still with its writing on it, from the fax machine. But he had written on both sides. So the whole performance had to be repeated. Alasdair watched in awe as his document started to disappear for a second time. Probably slightly less apprehensive this time, as he had seen it re-emerge once already.

"That's it done. Your text is now in New York."

"Ah."

Alasdair took his sheet of foolscap back, paid his fee, said thank you and quietly left the office, almost in a trance.

I was waiting outside just around the corner at the top of Kelvingrove Park.

"Well, how did it go?"

"Unbelievable! Unbelievable! Sheer magic! And it hasn't eaten up my paper. There's a duplicate of it in

America. It's amazing the things you find up here in Park Circus. Isn't Park Circus an incredible magical place!"

We walked on, strolled around the park, then off to the Chip for a couple of drinks.

The Anderston decantment

Towards the end of the 1980s came the Anderston decantment. Alasdair was decanted from the huge flat that he had occupied in Kersland Street, in the West End of Glasgow, because the City Council had decided that they needed to do the flat up, it was in such a state, a real state. I was surprised that it hadn't gone on fire before then. The electrics were in such a bad way. And also, unbeknown to Alasdair at the time, the Council wanted to divide the place up into individual flats. So they decanted him, and I think that, although a part of Alasdair thought that he would get an equivalent sort of flat eventually, deep down he knew that would never happen. A "forced flitting" he called it.

He was a single man at this point, his first wife Inge and son Andrew having moved out, after the break-up of the marriage, and artistic needs did not feature near the top of the Council's housing assessment criteria. So he was allocated to Anderston, to a place like a prison block, a grey, depressing building, in which he was moved into a sort of maisonette type of place, a horrid little flat with tiny little rooms. There was no room

Alasdair stayed in a flat in the building on the left.

to do any artwork at all, no room for what was really important to him. I visited him there a few times, when he tried to sketch me for the book *Something Leather*, the initial idea for which we'd thought up together. And he did a sketch of my face, to the side, to the front.

"May, I need to make you bald in this picture."

What was all that about? So I had to draw my hair right into my head so that he could get the shape of it. And it was during one of my visits, when we were discussing relationships, that he told me that one of the characters in the book, called Donalda, was going to be someone he'd met.

"I've met this woman. I met her in the Chip. Her name's Morag. She's a bookseller and she works in John Smith's and she really likes me."

"That's really nice," I said.

I think by this time he had come to accept that our relationship was platonic. It took him a long time to believe that. Can I be really sure that he did believe it? I can't, no.

And he said Morag and him were getting along really well, and he was going to… he was thinking about… moving. Because she'd asked him to move into her flat.

"Where is it she lives?"

"Oh, you'll never guess, you'll just never guess where she lives."

"No, I probably won't."

"She lives near you. She lives just next door to you!"

"That's nice," I said. "We'll be handy for each other."

And then he showed me a little drawing he'd done of her and I recognised her face because Morag (I'm not being cruel) Morag had quite a round little face and I sort of recognised it as a cartoon.

I said, "That's my neighbour."

And he said yes. He knew she was my neighbour. But I didn't know, I didn't know then that he was becoming involved with her.

I was actually taken aback. I just thought that kind of closeness, and realising how drunk he could get, I did worry a bit about that, if he was living so close to me.

But in the Anderston flat he was very, very unhappy, I mean totally miserable, because he couldn't carry on with his artistic work, his painting and writing. Even when he'd draw me, the pad had to be on his knee and that wasn't the way he did things as a rule. And he was drinking far too much and had become friends with several of the neighbours, who had equal alcohol problems, and frequently they could all be found in a heap in the morning, having all got really drunk overnight. All in a heap in Alasdair's little flat. And people were getting very worried about Alasdair being in Anderston. Because he was just going downhill. His artistic life was in trouble, banging up against a barrier. Alasdair was quite a lone worker, although he did work a lot with the Print Studio. But in his head, and when he was painting or when he was writing, he was always on his own, and he needed room, there had to be space. If you're an artist you have to have space. I'm into art now and I find my flat far too small and yet it's twice the size of the room in Anderston, at least twice the size. And he was so unhappy there. And I suppose Morag came along like, I don't know if you can describe a woman as a knight, a knight in shining armour, and kind of saved him. So she did, she did save him. I wonder sometimes what would have happened if he'd stayed there. I think he would have died. I do, because he was drinking so much, I mean he always did drink a lot, but in the Anderston flat he was really downing it. I think he would have drunk himself to death. So in a way I have a lot to thank Morag for.

The Fairy Falls

Alasdair relaxing at the hut

I have a hut out in the countryside, in Carbeth (it's called a hut but it has two bedrooms, living room, huge kitchen, bathroom, wood burner). There are fences and privet hedges all the way around. Although there are other huts in the area there is a great feeling of privacy and seclusion here. Alasdair absolutely loved going there and it was brilliant to get him out of his Anderston prison.

One fine day, in the early 1990s, my partner Robert drove Alasdair and me out to the hut. The menfolk had decided a walk was in order, although I would have been quite happy just to sit there and read. So off we went. We cut across some fields as there was no path then; this was before the John Muir Trail was established. Our destination was the Kilmannan Reservoir, so we headed towards the Old Kilpatrick Hills and followed the trail down to what is known as the Old Murroch Burn. It was a beautiful day and the sun was shining. It was summer and it was warm. Alasdair was just revelling in being out in the open air under a big sky with the hills rolling away in the distance.

He loved walking. And he was a fast walker, usually leaving me behind, beavering along with his little quick short steps, sometimes tripping, stumbling, not often falling (he saved that for when he'd had a few). To lose his mobility years later had to be devastating and when I think about his love of walking, I find it quite distressing.

I thought Alasdair would like to see the Fairy Falls, a place he had never been to before. As we approached the Falls, Alasdair became more animated than usual when he saw the crash of the waterfall onto the stones.

We told him there was also a steep man-made route down to the Fairy Falls and suggested we should try it so that he could get the full experience. To do this we would have to climb up to the top of the Falls. It wasn't easy, but he was keen to have a go, so we used the steep path, slithering down. And he was delighted.

Eventually, when we arrived back down at the banks of the pool of the Fairy Falls, we sat for a while and Alasdair took out his sketchbook and began sketching the Falls. He had rolled up his sleeves and his arms were getting red. Knowing that he had a skin condition (and therefore a life of creams), I took out my sunscreen.

"Alasdair, give me your arm."

He was happy to do this. But then he saw the sunscreen coming.

"No, I don't want that. No cream." He was clearly annoyed now but went back to his sketching, problem over.

Walking back, following the course of the Murroch Burn, heading towards the huts just off the Drymen Road, yet again despite this being a sunny day, no stile this time, Alasdair managed to step into a boggy area, part of the Murroch Burn and once more his shoe (this time a sandal) became a casualty. Robert retrieved the sandal and washed it in the stream. Alasdair took off his muddy wet sock and wrung it out. He put the wet sandal and muddy sock back on and we continued our walk.

Although it could not have been comfortable, he didn't complain.

"This is becoming a habit!" he hooted.

We walked on, following the burn, passing the only hut on that side of the water. Alasdair told us that his father once owned a hut in that area and pointed to the place where it had stood, but now long since demolished. Alasdair was pointing to the area near the Carbeth Fisheries.

We returned to our hut and after sketching and reading in the garden I suggested it would be a good idea to go to the Carbeth Inn. Sadly, the inn is no longer there, well the bones of it remain. There is no roof and the building has been partially demolished. I had the idea that they would rebuild it since I'm pretty sure it's a listed property, but they haven't followed through.

Of course, that idea of going to the inn appealed to Alasdair, as he liked nothing more than a wee refreshment. We reached the main road where there was no safe place to cross and still isn't, so we (or rather Robert and I) carefully assessed the traffic, it's a blind corner, so we walked a little further and crossed at the Stockiemuir Road area where the traffic can be seen more clearly. (Alasdair would almost certainly just have wandered across the road.) We went into the inn and had some drinks. He drank his usual several whiskys (*a Scottish spelling, that's how Scottish whisky is identified, not the -ies plural ending please, Alasdair was very particular about this*). We sat outside on the benches; and he was a sight to behold wearing his blue tank top and a straw hat to shield him from the sun, looking every bit the artist. We discussed his current thoughts about writing. As usual, he became excited, his voice getting louder and louder until he was declaiming, up on a soapbox, talking to everyone within a range of 100 yards, but delighting us and others at the inn, causing them some amusement, but no one was upset, he was so agreeable.

Morag and the move to Marchmont Terrace

efore Alasdair arrived on the scene at Marchmont Terrace, which was sort of serendipitous, or not – depends on how you look at it – I only knew Morag in passing. A nodding acquaintance. I would say good morning or good afternoon. I would see her sometimes in her ground-floor window. She had a habit of looking out of her window to see passers-by. And she used to live with another man, who shared the flat with her. The two of them would stand looking out of the window a lot. And I would see him occasionally, and then for some reason or another they split up. And then she lived alone. And that's really all I knew, I didn't know anything about her. Who she was, what she did or what she was like. I would say hello, how are you? I knew nothing, and I only recognised her as the woman who Alasdair was involved with after he had shown me the picture he had drawn of her while he was still living in the horrid little Anderston hellhole.

I just thought, this is strange. Because I've lived in this terrace, Marchmont Terrace, since I moved here in 1984 and this is the nineties. And Alasdair has visited me here in my flat many times. And now he is moving here to live with Morag. And there was a bit of me thought, is your relationship with Morag developing (and this is horrid of me, and it's not how I think generally) is this more to do with me than Morag? I don't know now. And I didn't know then, and I'll never ever know. I had to wonder, would he have moved in with Morag if she had lived out of town or out in the suburbs? Maybe everything was coming together for him, moving back to the West End.

Anyway, he moved in with Morag in Marchmont Terrace. And I was like, "What?!" We are on the same street, we are three doors apart. There are no closes on Marchmont Terrace. It's only 1 – 10, it's a very short terrace. And I'm at Number 5 and he's in Number 2. I didn't think Morag was his type. I didn't really understand it. But then, when I met her, got to know her a bit, I knew she kind of was his type, because she was controlling, very much like Bethsy, very much like Inge. So he certainly had his type.

"I'll have space to paint," said Alasdair.

Because there's a huge big front room. And he was delighted; you've got to remember, he was in a tiny little flat in Anderston, where you couldn't swing a cat. The front room there was a quarter the size of his old bed-room in Kersland Street, you couldn't put an easel in it or anything, and it really wasn't conducive to writing either. And I feel kind of horrid about saying this, but there was a bit of me that couldn't help wondering if it was a great move for him just because he would have space. Or were there other reasons? Anyway, I could be completely wrong.

But I thought, well good, if he's happy. As I said, I didn't really know Morag very well. But I thought, well she must be nice enough. And when he moved in and we kept in contact I would visit frequently, or infrequently, depending on Morag's mood. She would ask me round, I'd go round, we'd sit and have a drink in front of a sort of gas fire, in a huge room and the room was bloody freez-ing. I had tartan legs sitting right beside the fire, you had to get right beside it. They did eventually get central heat-ing. Alasdair told me that they had got a grant to put in central heating – best thing that ever happened because that house was like a freezer. It was so cold.

And so before I knew it Alasdair had moved into Marchmont Terrace and seemed to be okay with Morag. And within a few years, I think it was just two, I can't be certain, of moving into the Terrace, I was out for a drink with Alasdair and he said something to me (and I do re-member his words because I was so taken aback).

"Well, Morag and I, we've been together a wee while now and she's asked me to marry her, and I can't think of a reason why not."

And those were his words. Some say that Alasdair proposed. He did not. She did. She suggested it.

And I said, "How on earth did that come about?"

"Well, she suggested we get married and I could see no reason why we shouldn't. It's not as if I'm getting any younger or I want to spend the rest of my life looking for someone that I'll never find."

Wedding day

And so Alasdair and Morag got married. They got married in Glasgow, in Martha Street Registry Office. Angela Mullane, a lawyer with whom years before he had set up the Dog and Bone Press, and who was known as the Angel of Drumchapel, was there as a witness and the other witness was meant to be his son, Andrew. But for one reason or another Andrew didn't show up. He had come all the way from America, had arrived in Glasgow, but didn't make it to the actual ceremony. And they found that out after the ceremony when they had had to get someone else to be the other witness – it was either a member of staff from Martha Street or someone plucked off the street. Alasdair was very upset. Which was awful, because, well, this is supposition – I believe that Andrew probably didn't want his dad to marry Morag. Andrew and Morag, I just know that they didn't get on.

Are you coming to my wedding, son?
It's a long long journey of thousands
of miles. But I hear you will be in
Glasgow at that time. And will you
be a witness when I marry Morag?
You will, so glad. So wonderful,
my son. Nothing can stop this now.
Surely nothing can stop this now. You
will be by my side. You will wish me
all happiness and joy, when you are
at my wedding to Morag, son. We
two together.

It was a long long journey across the Atlantic, son. And back to the Glasgow which you left behind you. You were to be my witness at the wedding, son. Were you not? But where are you now? Are you close by? Shall we wait a little longer? Angela is here already. She is one witness to my marriage, my second marriage. My marriage to Morag. Do not let thoughts of your mother hold you back. Please do not let Inge hold you back. Dear Inge. Poor Inge. It has been a long long journey, son. You must be close. But we cannot wait. Our time has been booked. We must go on without you, son. Can you not wish us happiness? Is the final act too much for you? My lovely boy.

Near neighbours

We visited each other quite often, both before and after their marriage. We would have drinks together, but Morag generally got annoyed with me, although she didn't say as much, but I could tell by her expression. And when Alasdair and I were in deep conversation she would tell him off for being boring, and I would never know what to do, because I didn't want any controversy, because I don't like that, I hate it. So we usually sort of got along alright, although I always felt I was treading on eggshells when Morag was there. But there was one thing Morag did, and this is what made me not too keen on her. Alasdair was a great story-teller, always telling stories, but he would go off at tangents. He'd be telling me one story, then go on to the next, and I would kind of be following it, but Morag would get angry with him, and because she was so irked I would lose track of the story.

"May doesn't want to hear that. You can be quite a bore sometimes, Alasdair. I'm sure May finds you just as boring as I do."

It's the sort of thing I might say to somebody, but I'd say it in private, I wouldn't say it in front of someone. And I never knew where to put myself, I could just feel my face getting redder and redder and redder! And he would sort of tut and apologise! He was quite apologetic, but not to me. He wouldn't apologise to me but he would to her.

"I'm sorry, Morag."

And then he would stop telling the story. And then he'd have another glass of whisky and then start again with the story-telling. So he wouldn't really stop for good. No, he would get quite frustrated though. You could see his face changing. He had an anxiety thing and his face would start to get red and he would start to stutter, but he never really fought tooth and nail with Morag. He tried not to argue back but would get really upset. Morag had the ability to make him stammer with anger.

"Wha wha wha what are you saying?" – that sort of thing and she would just sort of shrug her shoulders at him. She was definitely in control. And I felt at a loose end. I really did. Quite often I left early.

"I have to go, I'm tired."

And then there was the thing about clothes. I occasionally gave Morag some clothes, because Morag always dressed abysmally. And I love clothes. So I would sometimes offer her some clothes.

"Look, I've got some clothes that I don't wear and I was going to give them to charity, would you like them?"

"Yes."

So I gave her some sweaters or stuff like that. My trousers were always far too long for her, she was very short, she was really short, about 4 foot 10 or something. And then when I gave her some of my clothes, we got on fine, we got on really well and I even occasionally had tea with her (she didn't drink coffee) when Alasdair wasn't in. But often, when Alasdair was there, she would lose it and it would be because of me, and I didn't know what I had done. Was she jealous of my closeness to Alasdair? And then when Alasdair died and I organised a night at the Òran Mór called *Loving Alasdair*, somebody said something to me.

"You know, Morag really hated you, May."

Someone felt they had the right to say that to me, and I just didn't think that was very nice. I think Morag might have said "I don't like her" but she didn't mind me, she didn't, because I was quite useful.

Neither Alasdair nor Morag had a television. Morag said televisions were evil. Alasdair said he didn't mind them too much and the reason he wouldn't have one was firstly because Morag would never have allowed him to have one, and secondly he couldn't have got on with his work, because he loved movies, so he didn't have one. But he always had a radio, he loved his radio.

The two of them would sometimes come around to my place. At this time I was producing a newsletter for a monthly stroke carers group that I had organised myself on a voluntary basis (for which I was given a Glasgow City Council Community Health Award). And Alasdair was really quite proud of this and sometimes edited my newsletter for me. But usually they came round to visit if there was a particular film that Alasdair wanted to see, and Morag would be accompanying him and drinks would be served, but the films were usually watched by me, Alasdair and Robert, and Morag would just get a little ansty.

"This is rubbish, this is rubbish," she would say.

But generally she just sat there drinking and I would make conversation, forgoing the film. When she wanted to leave, with the stress on the 'want', the actual leaving was not so straightforward, because by this time she would be paralytic. I can think of a few occasions when that poor man, Robert, who didn't keep in good health himself, had to physically put her over his shoulder and carry her home. And I'm three up, remember... And she was three doors away. Luckily on the ground floor. Anyway, he's a good, kind man is Robert and didn't really mind. But he'd be exhausted by the time he came back.

"Never again!" he'd say. But of course he did.

So often Alasdair would come up to my place on his own and he and Robert would watch a film together. Sometimes all three of us would watch together but generally it was the two of them. And during their first few years on the Terrace Alasdair and Morag would first-foot us every Hogmanay. They would come up, and I really loved that, but I knew that generally one of them would need help to get home – usually Morag. Alasdair was so used to being drunk but Morag couldn't really handle her drink. I don't know why she drank so much, because she got drunk really quickly, so that was that.

I remember once asking Alasdair why he drank so much.

"Because it makes me feel stupid." That was the unexpected answer, which I didn't believe.

On some occasions Alasdair would come up to see me while my mother was there. Mum was a nippie sweetie. A former nurse, now in her retirement, she had developed a horrendous facial cancer. But she had warmed to Alasdair by this time, no longer seeing him as only a wild eccentric artist and boozer, as she had done when they first met beside my hospital bed. He was a caring, concerned person and asked after her health and was incredibly sympathetic to her. He showed a lot of interest in the failed medical interventions. The two of them got on really well and could chatter away, although with Mum being almost completely deaf at this time, Alasdair had to raise his voice more than a little, not a problem for Alasdair, who was a natural voice-projector (as anybody who has ever been in the same pub as him, or in his company, would easily understand).

And Alasdair loved coming up to my third-floor flat to see the views. To get the best view he would climb into the loft space and go out through the sky-light and out onto the roof. Well, it was a valley roof, which decreased the risk of falling off, but my heart was always in my mouth when he did this. What could he see? He could see the lie of the land, the shape of the city, the buildings in the West End, the curves of Park Circus, Glasgow University Tower, the Campsies to the north and the Clyde to the south with the cranes and Govan on the other side. He loved the panorama. And he could see the spire of the Lansdowne Church (about which I would get a full commentary).

When I went round to their place it was really just a visit. It wasn't generally to see Morag, although that sounds quite mean, it was just to see Alasdair. Just because I was his friend. There didn't need to be a reason. I was his friend and he mine. We just had a blether.

As often as not it would be Morag who came to the door. I've never met anybody else who would answer the door in such a state of undress as Morag did. And I know I wasn't the only one to experience the full Morag. Alasdair's poor assistants would sometimes go in into the flat in the morning to begin work and both Morag and Alasdair would still be drunk, often answering the door half-naked. His assistants would find it difficult to cope, unable to hide their embarrassment but wanting to begin work. Alasdair could usually pull himself together, but Morag was a different story, often going back to bed and pulling the covers over herself then getting up and setting off for Tennent's pub to begin all over again.

Morag kept a kitchen cupboard stacked to the gunnels with signed copies of her husband's books which she would sell to anyone who came to the flat; and she let it be known in the West End of Glasgow that she had signed copies for sale.

So that's the story of the move to Marchmont Terrace, which to me was the most bizarre thing in the whole wide world, because I had met Alasdair when I lived on the other side of the river on Paisley Road West. I'd kept in touch with him over the years when he was in Kersland Street in the West End; and suddenly he was my neighbour. And people, when they read about me – because I was in a couple of newspaper articles after he died where I am simply referred to as his "friend and neighbour" – it's as if I only knew him because of being a neighbour. And that is not the reason. I often think, was

it by chance that we had become neighbours? Or was it not by chance? I don't know. And yes, he stayed on in that flat. There was no more moving after that. It was a nice big flat. The ground floor was really big.

Alasdair and Morag fought a lot. Nobody really knows much about their relationship. You'd think they were this gorgeous couple. But Morag certainly did not get on with Andrew, Alasdair's son. Not at all, so she made a decision, and even though I thought she sort of disliked me, she did confide in me.

"May, I have made my will, and Andrew's not getting it, Andrew's not getting my flat. I'm leaving it to my two nieces."

And she kept her word, and her will stated quite clearly that Alasdair could live in her flat until his death and then the flat would pass to her nieces, and Alasdair agreed with her wishes, and Andrew did not get the flat. She didn't even like him being in the flat. It's not that she wouldn't let him in, but she didn't like him being there if she wasn't there as well so that she could control the situation.

The Abbot's House

"You'll never guess what Alasdair did today!" Robert, my partner, had just that minute arrived back in Glasgow from across the country in Dunfermline, where he had been working as Alasdair's assistant on a new mural. What a thrill for Alasdair: a commission to create a wall and ceiling mural in the Abbot's House in Dunfermline, a building dating back to the 16th century, and with parts going even further back into the Middle Ages and set close by the Abbey, the resting place of ancient Scottish kings. For a man with such a passion for Scottish history and so broad a grasp of it (this was something which he could and would talk about for hours on end), a commission like this was a gift from heaven. Excited? Proud? That came nowhere near his state of mind. Here he was, in with the history.

Well, there's a few wee stories about the Abbot's House but I'm just going to give you a taste.

The historic house was in a sorry state of disrepair but, for this reason, it presented a blank canvas of opportunity, its walls and ceilings crying out for vibrant murals depicting legends and people that had shaped the area.

Alasdair, alongside his trusted assistant and companion, Robert Salmon, who'd also helped him with several other commissions, was determined to bring the House back to a state that did justice to its past. He first intended to create a history tree but then opted for a thistle with roots and thistle heads instead. The thistle heads, like speech bubbles, representing many important events that had taken place in Dunfermline. And there were many prominent people associated with the Abbot's House, people who had benefitted the area and were well known. The portraits of the historical figures, of the kings and queens and bishops and monks and others, were all based on Alasdair's own friends and acquaintances. Because who knew what these people really looked like? Alasdair also used faces of the craftsmen who were there working on the building at the same time.

The two began work on the mural in the summer of 1994 and the work would take over a year to complete. They toiled for hours, week after paint-splattered week, driven by aesthetic passion and the need to see the work through to completion.

But the work there was not exactly without its complications.

Robert and Alasdair were painting on the ceiling with silver aluminium paint – painting lines around leaves and such. Alasdair tilted his head while focusing on the ceiling, causing the tin to tip over and paint to pour onto his face, beard and clothes. The paint also splashed onto a life-size suffragette wax model and covered a large area of the floor. Robert spent some time cleaning up the model until it returned to its original state (this was an expensive piece of work, and the museum organisers would not have been pleased if it had not been done promptly – I doubt if they ever found out to this day). Alasdair himself held back from the cleaning operation. Robert gave Alasdair rags to clean his face. This was silver aluminium, so it was difficult to remove, and Alasdair tried to remove it with white spirit, but his beard remained mostly silver, and he smelled of turps. He had to go to the bathroom to wash his face and shampoo his beard. Robert was concerned about the spirit being so near his mouth, but Alasdair was unconcerned and simply let the silver paint dry on his overalls. His beard remained silver for about a week afterwards.

Alasdair spent the daytimes painting and at night he'd be drinking. Well, one night his wife, Morag, visited Dunfermline, basically, I believe, to see what he was up to. Alasdair and Morag were both heavy, heavy drinkers and on this night, when the painting work was done for the day, all three of them – Alasdair, Robert and Morag – went out for a curry and then on to the pub and the Grays got really blootered.

The Abbot's House staff had closed up the Abbot's House. It's a museum type of place with valuable artefacts. They locked it up for the night and everyone thought that the mural painters had gone home or gone to their digs.

After the pub Alasdair and Morag went back to the Abbot's House (one of them had a key) and yet more whisky was drunk.

Now in the room where the mural was being created there was a very old big bed, in which in bygone times all the lords and ladies, all the dukes and duchesses had slept, an antique bed with a canopy. Alasdair and Morag chose to sleep in this antique bed. This relic from centuries past, which had likely cradled royalty, was a narrow space, yet it was into this bed that Alasdair and Morag clambered and went to sleep.

"I, the Earl of Riddrie and Blackhill, now with thee, my most beauteous and virtuous consort, the Lady Morag of Marchmont, shall most pleasurably take me to my bed and may sweet dreams of perfect bliss come upon us."

Is that what he really said? Very probably. Or something similar.

Come the morning and the Abbot's House was opened again and a group of visitors were being shown around. As they explored, they stumbled upon Alasdair and Morag just waking up in the bed that was part of the museum's exhibits. Under the top cover, but completely naked beneath it. Robert was with the visiting party and swiftly intervened, highlighting in a diversionary sort of way the progress that had been made with the mural work and ushering the party off to another area. The visitors were embarrassed and relieved to be moved on and the people who had organised the visit were embarrassed too. But Alasdair and his wife were unperturbed, showing no concern at all. Back to work again.

Alasdair was painting many individuals associated with the Abbot's House Trust (The Carnegie Trust) and on one wall he had depicted one of the female volunteers working with the Trust, a local resident, I believe. It was a portrait with which he was especially pleased, one of his best ones.

Two women, exuding an air of snootiness, entered the House. The portrait bore a striking resemblance to a woman known to these two visitors and became their centre of attention, as they gathered around it. These two hoity-toity types seemed to be jealous.

"What is SHE doing on the wall?" they demanded.

Alasdair had chosen to depict as many subjects as the area could hold and there were a vast number of people associated with the Abbot's House, but the space available was limited and not everybody could be included.

"I think that looks like…," the women said scornfully.

Alasdair's response was sharp and loud.

"IT IS!"

The room crackled with tension. The women, embodying entitlement, again objected.

"We want it painted out!"

They actually wanted the image painted out! Alasdair was upset and refused their request.

"But it's some of my best work."

But they pressed on with their demand to have it removed.

Alasdair, unable to contain his fury, erupted into a fit of rage, he grabbed a Stanley knife and attacked the painting, slashing this way and that, plaster exploding into the air.

His voice resonated through the room as he gouged deep marks into the walls.

"THERE! ARE YOU HAPPY NOW!?"

Alasdair was bellowing, crimson in the face. In the chaos, two portraits were obliterated beyond repair.

His words echoed the anguish he felt. He stood, now pale, shaking and silent, his eyes filled as he trudged away, broken.

The women looked afraid, having witnessed the destruction they'd brought about. Alasdair's loyal assistant, Robert, led them out, his voice trembling.

"Do you see what you've done?"

Alasdair was visibly shaken and couldn't continue his work for the rest of the day, deeply upset. Silence settled over the Abbot's House as the women walked away and realised they had gone too far. The culmination of this interaction destroyed days of meticulous work and all because of jealousy and Alasdair's difficulties controlling his emotions.

All the artwork had been commissioned by the Carnegie Trust for the Abbot's House, with some finance also coming from the Dunfermline Building Society, likely amounting to thousands of pounds – for work that had been destroyed.

There was now the daunting task of repairing the damage. Alasdair had Robert fill in the holes and prepare the wall, instead of repainting the portraits. On this newly prepared surface Alasdair then placed a panel on which he painted words telling the story of the Abbot's House.

Other people's food

It was probably in 2000, because Alasdair had never been greedy before that, not that I remember – apart from the Buttery incident when it was nouvelle cuisine – I was starving after that as well. I'll tell you about that later. Alasdair had leg ulcers and Morag was forever trying to make him lose weight and she would put him on very very low-fat diets, which I disagreed with, but nobody could disagree with Morag because she knew it was the best. But nobody on a low-fat diet can survive for too long because the impulse to eat takes over and low-fat diets don't satiate you, fats satiate you, your brain needs it anyway. But she couldn't see that, and I couldn't get her to see that. When I met him he was always hungry. It was a bloody shame, it really was! He was always hungry, and I do remember saying to Morag that I would make something and occasionally I took something I'd cooked down to their place, and it'd be tasty. Yes, there would be some fats in it, but it would be minimal because I knew she wouldn't eat it, she would eat things like chicken and she would tear the skin off – really tasteless. So I would maybe take down a lamb stew or something like that, and he loved it, he did, he loved it. And the three of us would eat together. And he would eat his food quite quickly and then he would point at my plate and say, "Do you want that, May?"

"No, you can have it, I've got more upstairs."

Which I did.

Then I would just pass him my plate. Poor hungry man! But Morag wasn't that keen because she wanted things like skinless chicken. I couldn't get it through to her what amino acids were and what essential fats were, I just couldn't. Anyway, I gave up on that one. But she was appreciative of me cooking things for them. I can't put her down. She was appreciative, but she knew what she knew and I didn't know anything.

So the result was that Alasdair overate the wrong things when he was out because he was hungry. He couldn't survive on skinless chicken, he couldn't do it. I understand people have got preconceptions about health, I absolutely do, but when someone is left hungry it doesn't work if you're trying to make them lose weight and they're hungry all the time, they are going to cave, they're completely going to cave. And I think that's what happened to Alasdair. He'd got a sort of caving side, an addictive side to him, so that if anything that did satiate him was there (which it never was, generally) he would want more of it.

One fine day many years later we were sitting on a bench by Loch Katrine where four of us had gone on an

outing, me, my cousin Pamela, Alasdair and with Robert driving. We were talking about this and that and the talk came round to Alasdair's biography. I asked him if he was still pleased with it.

"Ha! Rodge Glass used to drive me bonkers with all his questions."

"But you did like having your biography written, didn't you? I mean it's not everyone who has a biography done for them."

"Oh yes. Rodge was my Boswell. But how was I supposed to remember all the little details and what happened when and whether this came before that or that came before this? I did my best, May. As I've said before, the past is always true. The past is the one thing we cannot change."

"We can only change the way we describe it."

"Mmm."

We then decided to go on a boat trip on the Sir Walter Scott. On the boat a voice came over the Tannoy.

"Does any of our passengers want to come up and take the wheel for a spell?"

Of course Alasdair was up for this and, double whisky in hand and slightly staggering, he took over the helm. Under close supervision by the crew, it goes without saying.

Back ashore, there was an ice cream kiosk nearby and I asked him if he wanted some ice cream, and he said yes, he would like an ice cream. And I had one as well. And before you could blink Alasdair's was finished while I was still licking mine, and I think I was doing it to annoy him as well, which was horrible of me, but I did know that I would give him it, and I did give him it and he willingly took it. He didn't actually ask for it but just looked, he looked over and I knew that he wanted it. Like a wee dog or like a wee boy. And that's okay.

Do you remember when you were wee and you saved up your sweets and your brothers or sisters would look at you? It was that kind of look. And I had more than them,

"Do you want the rest of that, May?"

well I'd more *left* than them, not more than them. It was a bit like that.

"You've got sweeties and I don't," that sort of thing.

And yes, I was going to tell you about the Buttery. That was hilarious.

He got an advance on a book (and don't ask me what book) it was something he'd got an advance for and he phoned me up in a state of high excitement.

"I have money! We can get a taxi to The Buttery. I heard it's very good."

And this is in the 80s and nouvelle cuisine was kind of all the rage – I've never understood why, never will. And so we went along. He didn't know what nouvelle cuisine was, he hadn't got a scoobie, and actually neither did I. So we ordered something that looked really nice when it came, and it was a little tiny piece of food on a plate, decorated like a flower with bits of I think they call it 'jus' going one way and the other, and it was beautiful, it was a work of art. However… It tasted lovely but you wanted twenty times that on your plate. Yeah, and I think it was very expensive, I don't remember exactly how much, but I think it was very very expensive and there was nothing to eat! It was like eating fresh air. And so we had that, and he looked a bit embarrassed because he'd taken me there. And of course Alasdair filled up with whisky. He ordered one whisky after the other. I didn't drink, I'd sort of given up drinking a bit by then, but I did go back on it, in fairness I went back on it for quite a long time. And we left and we were going back to the West End.

"Are you still hungry, May?"

"Actually, I am."

"Let's go and get a fish supper!" said he.

And so we did, we just got one between us though, because we'd already had something. But who do you think took most of the chips, leaving just a few for me? No problem, I was absolutely fine with that. The main thing was that Alasdair should be happy. And full.

Inge comes to stay

I got a call from Morag, not Alasdair, to say that Alasdair's wife had arrived. His first wife had arrived, Inge, and she had already said that she was coming to visit and Morag wasn't happy about it but she accepted it, reluctantly, knowing Morag. And then when Inge arrived at the door it was clear that she was very unwell and it was obvious that she wasn't going anywhere once she'd moved into the flat. She was that unwell.

She arrived and because Alasdair's Alasdair and Morag was his wife, and she loved Alasdair in her own way, I have no doubt, Morag admitted Inge to the flat. I think had Inge been well she wouldn't have got over the door. But Inge was unwell and she went into their flat and she couldn't do much for herself. She was dying, she'd been diagnosed with terminal cancer, but they didn't know that.

She had come up from down south, I think it was from London. She came to Glasgow, to visit the Grays, and she wanted to stay there, but she didn't want to sleep on the settee, because she wasn't well, so basically she asked to have their bed. Now Alasdair and Morag had a one bedroom flat and they did not have a bed-settee, so Alasdair and Morag had to sleep on a mattress on the floor while she took their bed. That's when I became involved. Morag phoned me up, really quite distraught.

"I don't know what to do, May. She's wanting a massage, she wants this, she wants that. I don't know what to do, I feel like screaming. Can you come down? I know you've been a nurse and have done massage training and I know you know things."

I'm thinking, what do I know? And I went down and Morag showed me into the room where Inge was lying.

"What can I do for you?" I asked.

"Well, I'd quite like my legs massaged, and my back, and if you could do my arms as well."

"I need to find out what's wrong with you first."

"Oh, I'm dying."

So I thought, well in that case I will give you a massage. And she wanted specific oils.

"Inge, I am going to have to go to my house to get these things and mix them, because I don't have them made up."

"That's fine."

There was no thank you, no nothing, and so I went and mixed all the oils up and I came back and just basically massaged her whole body, very gently because I didn't want to upset her equilibrium, because she was in pain. I did that for her.

131

"I'm settled now," she said.

And at that particular time Morag had managed to get out of the house to go a walk and I think she went to the pub, to Tennent's, I'm pretty sure she did, she practically lived in Tennent's. So I had done what Inge asked and I left. It was Alasdair who thanked me not Inge. And that was nice, because I didn't need a thank you from Alasdair. I needed a thank you from her, but I didn't get one. And I did that a couple of times and then, because Morag had been in touch frequently, which she never was normally, because there was this thing between us, not with me but Morag wasn't sure if she liked me, Morag wanted things done and nothing was happening. By that time I was a social worker, working in community care.

"Can you call someone so that we can get an assessment done of what her care needs are?" asked Morag.

"Yes, I can do that."

So I contacted the Social Work Department and explained the concerns and was told that a social worker would be in touch to arrange a home visit to assess the situation. But Inge had decided that she really can't get out of bed again and she wants the bed, but is also saying she's scared and wants Alasdair to sleep with her to make sure she has someone there. To sleep in the same bed with her. Morag was really upset, totally distressed.

But it happened. Inge got her way. There's no more I can say about that, I wasn't privy to what went on after that except I knew Morag was really unhappy. And that's really all I can say about that.

So for a couple of weeks Alasdair shared a bed with his first wife and during this time Morag would sleep on a mattress on the floor. She was quite small actually, so she could have used the little settee but she'd probably have ended up on the floor…

Both Morag and Alasdair were at the ends of their tethers. Morag more so than Alasdair. And Alasdair? Alasdair did not know which wife to please. At some stage Inge's son, Andrew, arrived in Glasgow to look after his mother. I then stepped back. Shortly afterwards Inge did leave the flat. And she died.

When Inge came back to Glasgow, Alasdair felt very sorry for her, but he also felt that she'd come back to manipulate him, as she'd done before. He just felt that she always, always had to have her own way and she was having it again.

But in a way she got her final comfort. She'd been married twice more, I think. So it's not as if she didn't have anywhere else to go. She did, and she had family in Denmark but she chose to come to Alasdair. There had to be something special in it. I don't know the ins and outs of it. Andrew, their son, might know the ins and outs.

*You weakling Alasdair, you coward, have
you no thought for how this will affect
Morag, how she will feel about this? Morag
is being destroyed. She is being pushed to the
outside. Does she not exist for you? Does she
not matter? Not matter at all? Do you expect
her to put up with all this? In her house? In
her own bed, for Christ's sake? There you
are, capitulating to the demands of a strong
woman. A woman who only wants to get
her own way. She has always used you. We
all know you were once convenient for Inge.
And now she wants to use you again. So you
just collapse, capitulate, offer no resistance.
You fool, you quivering coward, you spineless
miserable wreck, you horrible creature, say
no to her, ok she says she's dying, aren't we
all going the same way, the past is gone, so
bury it, send her out, don't let a ghost come
back, why should she overpower the living,
Alasdair what are you destroying, what are
you doing, you're weak, weak, Alasdair weak
despicable man you are.*

Who can say what the state of mind
was that lay behind all this, what the
motivation, does there even need to be
a motivation, do we not just sometimes
simply act the way we have to, follow
the only path that is there for us, are you
calling this cowardice, are you calling this
weakness, others might call it strength,
others might say you have risen above
the demands of pure self-interest, have
put down self and selfishness, have taken
in a soul in pain, a wanderer from out
your old life, one in pain, you have offered
comfort when comfort was asked for, when
comfort was needed before a life came to its
end, warm smoothness you once called it
yourself, you poet, what does the thinking
matter poet, too much thinking, too many
hurts, too many clashing hurts, what's left,
what happens, what is actually done is
loving kindness, loving kindness Alasdair
you hero you piece of genuine humanity
you.

Family involvement

I had gone down to Number 2 one evening to make a meal for Alasdair, Morag and my niece, Jennifer. She was doing a work experience placement with him at the time and he had invited her home for supper, Alasdair not being your typical employer. Alasdair was talking quite excitedly about how they were getting on in the Chip.

I recently reminded Jennifer of this time and she sent me a letter.

Hello Aunty May,

28th February 2024

Thanks for getting in touch and letting me know about the book you're writing about your times with Alasdair. You asked me if I remember the time I spent with him and of course I do! I'll tell you a wee bit about what I remember, especially about our week in the Ubiquitous Chip.

It was when I would have been about nineteen and at college doing art and design. It was actually a digital art and design course, but I was more interested in the practical and fine arts side of things. I had the opportunity of a work experience placement and since I was lucky enough to have known Alasdair, because obviously he was very good friends with you, it was with Alasdair that I got to do my placement. So I had a week's work experience working with Alasdair and Robert, renovating and re-touching his mural on the stairwell of the Chip, Ronnie Clydesdale's place. And it was a great experience in so many ways. Alasdair was very kind and very funny, but he was also extremely particular. For example, about how he wanted the brushes and paints handled and what were the mixing techniques that he liked. I learned a fair bit in that week, even though to be honest I spent the whole week pretty much just doing the one thing, which was touching up the peacock feathers. I mixed about a hundred different shades of blue – each one of these Alasdair liked and then thought not quite right, asking me to tweak this way and that – until he finally settled on one that I would swear was the exact same as the first blue I mixed.

So I spent that week touching up the blue sections of the peacock tails and it was a brilliant week. For one thing – and very importantly for nineteen-year-old me – it was supposed to be an unpaid work experience, but Alasdair paid me every day. On top of that, he took me to the pub at the end of most days, for food and drinks. I loved these times as he would regale me with many an entertaining tale.

Alasdair was just generally very very lovely. Hilarious. He spent most of the time while we worked telling tales, laughing and farting, not necessarily in that order.

One thing that really sticks out for me is the time he told me the story of how he came to watch a particular film. This story took quite a while because he was laughing the whole way through the telling. I can't exactly remember the place he was speaking of, but I think it was some new town like maybe like Cumbernauld? Or somewhere like that. He said that he was there to do a book reading and he had time to kill, so he and a friend – I'm told it was the writer Alan Bissett – went to the cinema and what was showing was Bedazzled: *that Brendan Fraser and Liz Hurley one with the careful-what-you-wish-for storyline.* And he just loved this movie. I remember being highly amused by this because here's this accomplished artist and author, this cultured man and he's just absolutely taken with this silly film. I can still picture him, jiggling with laughter as he tells me all about the plot. At nineteen I was still taking myself a bit too seriously and seeing how Alasdair could appreciate that kind *of film was instructive for me. He just thought it was a jolly good romp. So I watched it! And, to this day, every time I see any reference to that film or hear of those two actors or even just see the little thumbnail of it when I'm scrolling through films to watch, I always think of him. And it makes me smile.*

I had a great time with Alasdair, and I consider myself extremely lucky to have completed the work experience with him and Robert. I'm so glad that I got to know him, not least of all because he was so different from what I would have otherwise assumed. I still saw him now and again for years after that, of course. As you know, I worked part time in Tennent's bar for a long time, right through my degree and postgrad, and Alasdair would come in fairly regularly. It was always nice to see him and hear his distinctive laugh ringing out. He invited me to his house for dinner once or twice as well, which I was honoured by. We would have a carry-out or you would come round with something to eat.

Alasdair was just always so kind, so funny, really down to earth... and honest! So honest. I remember that he just couldn't help himself from commenting on my back tattoo because he couldn't believe I didn't have him design it. But it never would have occurred to me that I could just have asked him to design it and I kick myself regularly that I didn't. I like my tattoo, but if it had been designed by Alasdair I think it would have just been that extra bit special. Unfortunately, I didn't know until after the fact that he would have been willing to do it, but, aye, what a lovely man. What more can I say about him? He was very encouraging. He wanted to include a poem of mine in his book for independence. It never happened, for various reasons, but just the fact that he was interested in doing it really was a huge confidence boost for me. He was really warm and encouraging, as well as impressive and inspiring. He's very much missed.

Good luck with the book!

Love you,

Jen.

The Òran Mór mural

Glasgow, like most Scottish cities and towns, is full of old churches. One fairly enormous one was the Kelvinside Parish Church at the corner of Great Western Road and Byres Road: disused, decaying and stuffed with dead birds and their droppings. But in years to come a church to achieve fame as the Òran Mór. And here's me again heading off down the hill to that old church with a bag of food. The big scaffolding's down now, so Health and Safety will allow me in. Cheese and ham sandwiches for my partner Robert and for Alasdair and sometimes for Martin, Robert's son, as well. A bagload of stuff for the mural men hard at work in there, flasks of hot water so they could make tea and coffee. The old church was baltic. But here comes Little Red Riding Hood.

Colin Beattie, a well-kent Glasgow businessman, had known Alasdair for years. And Alasdair was quite famous as a mural painter. A much earlier mural of his had been demolished along with the old Bridgeton church it breathed life into when that church itself was razed to the ground. And Alasdair was known locally as the artist who, many years before, had painted the mural in the Ubiquitous Chip pub just a little way further down Byres Road. Colin and Alasdair had met in one of Colin's pubs, the Liosmor (or Lismore), a place where artists and writers gathered and drank. In or around 2003 Colin completed negotiations for the purchase of the church on Byres Road and began undertaking some massive renovation work in order to turn it into a theatre, restaurant with bars and reception areas. But what to do with the old church ceiling and walls, all cold and bare? Colin had a general sort of idea in mind; Alasdair went to him with suggestions; they began to click; soon after Alasdair presented a sample of his plan for a huge ceiling mural; Colin loved the idea; and they agreed to go ahead.

"Alasdair, what shall we pay you for the work?"

An hourly rate was offered.

"That's fine. As long as all my assistants get the same too."

Alasdair, the master of the mural work, wouldn't accept a rate of pay any higher than what his assistants were paid. So everyone in this whole undertaking got the same rate of pay. Them and us became just us.

Before the mural project could begin, some fairly major structural alterations had to be made to the ceiling. It had to be smoothed out and treated so as to be able to take the paint; and areas had to be created to serve as

the canvas for Alasdair's artwork. But how to reach the ceiling? A massive bird's-nest scaffold, some sixty foot high, was erected so that the mural artists could get right up to ceiling height, clambering up a series of near-vertical ladders to do their work that involved crouching, kneeling or lying at odd angles to paint. Alasdair had (or showed) no fear of heights, so up he went: quite a feat for the self-described "fat Glasgow pedestrian" (not long after a small heart attack too).

Alasdair was not alone in the mural work. He put together a team of painters, including Robert Salmon, Robert's son Martin, Richard Todd, Nichol Wheatley, Fergus Russell and Stef Gardiner. Stef was later to join Alasdair at home as his assistant.

Despite grappling with not insignificant health issues, Alasdair would clamber up and down the scaffold ladders, ensuring everything was matching his vision. He was a driven man, a perfectionist and everything had to fit together.

"No no, that line's wrong" or similar was often heard.

Alasdair meticulously sketched out designs, adjusting and getting the sizes just right. He was very particular about this. When necessary, he would get his drawings enlarged so as to ensure complete accuracy. He'd send someone from his team to the print shop to get enlargements of his drawings. The Òran Mór joiners working on the renovation helped by precision cutting hardboard templates. The outlines of the drawings would then be transferred onto the ceiling with white pencil.

There was also collage work where he would stick the prints to the wall and paint over them once pasted on.

Colin observed Alasdair's humanity and sensitivity, describing him as a "charm", innocent yet prolific once he began working. Colin was incredibly supportive throughout, giving Alasdair complete freedom in his designs. Some images produced were truly remarkable, including copulating skeletons and a detailed depiction of a baby being born, complete with umbilical cord. Themes of life and death and rebirth.

Alasdair's figures, the faces in the murals, reflected all those who contributed to the project, not just his own team. He showed his appreciation for their efforts by portraying them in the mural. So builders, plasterers, joiners, electricians as well as kitchen staff and office personnel are all immortalised.

During his time at the Òran Mór, Alasdair earned the affectionate nickname "Ali G", which he wholeheartedly embraced. The Ali G nickname originated from Martin Salmon. Alasdair loved it, although he had not the slightest idea what the reference was.

"Well, who is this Sacha Baron Cohen?"

Anyway he had another nickname for himself.

"I'm Honest Al, the punters' pal," he chuckled.

Alasdair also created his own unique font, which was used on both the ceiling and tiles of the project. He also crafted this font in metal, mainly making it visible on the beams within the gallery area. The hand-painted lettering was done by Robert Salmon.

The mural work first got off the ground when the building renovation work was already in full swing. Not unsurprisingly there was a bit of friction between the mural artists and some of the builders and decorators, although Alasdair himself was in general oblivious to this. One of the scaffolders would sometimes make snarky remarks about Alasdair's age and presence on the scaffolding.

"What's he doing up there? He's too old."

With the decorators there could be moments of professional pique.

"That's rubbish they're doing up there." Some of the tradesmen working on other jobs didn't fully understand the intricacies of mural work and may have felt excluded or threatened by their perceived lack of involvement.

And builders' and plasterers' dust floating up in the air would sometimes mean that painting had to be redone.

Alasdair's wife, Morag, would call him daily, but since Alasdair didn't have a mobile phone (he refused to own one), the calls went to Robert, asking to speak to

Alasdair. Morag usually called from Tennent's bar, where she spent a lot of time with others, and her lover, doing crosswords. The calls would come around 5.00pm, when mural work was finishing for the day. Sometimes Robert couldn't answer. Then Morag would call the Òran Mór staff instead.

"Tell her I'm not here."

A couple more drinks with the boys was what he really wanted now. But eventually, when she persisted, he would hurry off in a bit of a nervous panic.

Of course, even the committed perfectionist can sometimes be led astray. One day it was discovered that there had been an event in the gallery area the night before and people had left partially filled or even full glasses of wine on the tables. Too much for Alasdair to resist. He had a good drink from the left-overs, together with bacon rolls from the bar, which was open by this time. He didn't go back up the scaffold after that, ending his day's work early.

When Alasdair was absent because of health reasons (leg problems), this posed challenges given his perfectionist nature. However the team could follow the detailed notes he provided to Robert Salmon, who collected them from Alasdair at home. As long as the team adhered to his specific instructions, they could continue the work.

Despite frustration, exhaustion and ill health (and writing too), Alasdair never gave up. Just very occasionally he would become disillusioned.

"I've had enough. I wish I'd never started." But he would calm down and carry on, his passion for the project always driving him to return to the task.

A visit one day from a Health and Safety Inspector did nothing to calm his frustration. Alasdair threw an absolute tantrum.

"I won't have that officious little Health and Safety man telling me what I can and can't do!"

"Alasdair, he's just doing his job."

"Is he now? Rrright, everybody out! We're going off the job now until this Health and Safety man sorts out this scaffold."

And a walkout was called. Just for the rest of that day. The master had spoken and everyone downed brushes and left the building.

But Alasdair still had more steam to let off. So he wrote a long letter to Colin, asking him to speak to the Health and Safety man. He wrote it and gave it to Robert to give to Colin, but then asked Robert not to send it, because the matter had been settled in the meantime and he didn't want to upset Colin.

Then since the scaffolding had been examined and adjusted, the team resumed their work the following day.

And the scaffolding itself was a bit of an issue. For two main reasons.

For one thing poor Alasdair was forever bumping into things, especially the scaffolding, giving himself nicks and cuts and abrasions. When he got home of an evening I'd go around to his place to patch him up with bandages and dressings as needed. Maybe this didn't happen every week, but it was regular enough.

And sometimes it was those beneath the scaffolding who could be in a risky spot. When calls of nature came, things could be tricky. Other, younger artists with stronger bladders could, when the call came, climb down the ladders to pay a visit to the ground-level toilet. And then back up again. Not so easy for the older master, who instead peed into a galvanised bucket, supplied for him specifically for this purpose. His type-2 diabetes meant that the call came quite frequently. You will be able to appreciate that it would be quite tricky to get the aim right.

The ceiling team would have the task of emptying the bucket on Fridays, or before any noticeable odour arose. This was done by one team member who would attach a long rope to the handle securely and lower the bucket to the ground where another team member would empty it. The team saw this as part of the job; they respected Alasdair and admired his drive. And I'm sure the same sort of arrangement existed for Michelangelo.

Painting work on the ceiling mural was still ongoing when the theatre area of the Òran Mór was already up and running. On one never-to-be-forgotten occasion a play below was interrupted by a thunderbolt from above. Suddenly, the auditorium fell silent as a thunderous crashing sound shattered the performance. All eyes turned upward to witness a rogue gardening stool come hurtling down, banging and clanging off the scaffold on its way down. The projectile clattered to the floor, leaving a hush of disbelief. That's when Alasdair himself peeked over the gallery edge, his voice slicing through the stillness with a sheepish "sorry" in a stage whisper. The bizarre interruption hung in the air for a beat before the entire audience, joined by the actors, erupted into raucous laughter.

The play carried on, but Alasdair had earned himself a fitting nickname that day – Bomber Gray – courtesy of the quick-witted David McLellan of the famous *A Play, a Pie and a Pint* events. An unforgettable scene that everyone remembers.

These days the old run-down disused church has become known as Alasdair Gray's Glasgow Sistine Chapel. The ceiling mural has spread down to walls, pillars and the ground outside. Work on these murals at the Òran Mór was never officially completed. But you wouldn't know it. After all, how do you complete perfection?

Double booking

I never saw him without a book in each jacket pocket; he would be annotating them; reading two books at the same time; holding a conversation with me while also reading a book and not getting confused.

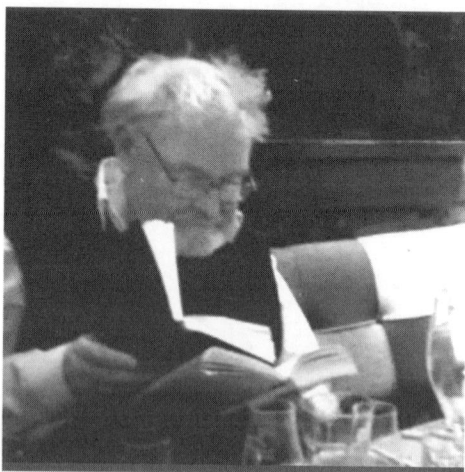

A Greek visitor

"Do you know, I had a visit from this young man, a Greek filmmaker."

"Really? Who was that?"

"His name is Yorgos Lanthimos. Think I've got that right. Anyhow it appears he is keen to turn *Poor Things* into a film. What do you make of that!"

"Never heard of him. Would it be a gothic movie or a sex film? Or a bit of both?"

"Well, I suppose that would be up to him."

"So was he down here with you? I'd've liked to meet him. I could have practised my Greek on him."

Alasdair just laughed.

"He didn't stay. I took him for a wee tramp around the Glasgow sights. And we went up to the Necropolis. He seemed to be struggling a bit to keep up, and he's only a youngster. I don't walk that fast, do I?"

"You can do, Alasdair. Is it all agreed then?"

"Yes, as far as I'm concerned he can go ahead and make the film. I let him know that. And I don't suppose the publishers will object."

"Tremendous. That's good news."

"And if you'd like to meet him, May, do you suppose he could bring his film people up to your flat? The views of Glasgow are so so good from up there. It would look rreally breathtaking, rreally stunning! I'd love to see all those sights in a film for the whole world to watch!"

Hillhead Subway

*B*its of a conversation overheard by a friend in Tennent's pub.

"OK if we sit here?"

"Aye, plenty of room."

"No murals in here then?"

"Eh? Na, jist a lot of fitba up on every wall."

"My wife and I have just been across the road at the Ubiquitous Chip. Great meal. But we were really there to look at the mural."

"Is that right? Where've ye come fae?"

"We're from Des Moines, Iowa. Here touring around Scatland. Loving it."

"Aye. Wit d'ye dae?"

"Pardon me?"

"What is your line of work?"

"Ah, we're both art teachers."

"Well, if ye tak the subway when ye leave here, ye'll see another mural. A right big one."

"Same artist?"

"Aye, it's by Alasdair Gray. But he wisnae the only one. There was Nichol that did a fair bit. Nichol Wheatley and some say he did most o' the work on it. The technical stuff. Cos it was that hard to get the images to stick on the tiles, near impossible, and it was Nichol got that all sorted. Without Nichol I doubt it would be there."

"We'll go across and take a look."

"Aye. And if ye hang on a wee bit, ye jist might see Alasdair himself in here. His wife's over there the noo, the wee woman wi' a' the newspapers spread oot on the table."

"We wouldn't want to interrupt her. Nice talking to you."

"Cheers."

Morag dies

It was in early 2014 that Alasdair told me that Morag was ill, that she was in increasing pain. For the first time ever, for the first time in his whole life, he said he was considering getting a private medical diagnosis. That is an indication of how upset he was. He was in tears telling me about it.

She was admitted to Gartnavel Hospital later that same year, just a few weeks after he had told me about the problem. She was diagnosed with cancer, which had reached a stage where it couldn't be treated. She didn't want any visitors towards the end because she could hardly eat and couldn't swallow. Alasdair would often lie beside her on the bed, but it was only a single hospital bed, although he asked for a bigger bed if possible. Of course, it wasn't possible. He stayed by her bedside until she died.

Robert and I went to the funeral, where Alasdair played Scottish songs and gave the eulogy. A hotel was booked in Cardross for the purvey. It was all very lovely actually.

After the funeral he became quite low and would visit me more frequently than he had done before. Without her he was lost. In spite of the untypical nature of their marriage, she had given him a level of security that he had never otherwise had. It was Morag that had paid the bills, organised the day-to-day matters.

Morag's will stipulated that Alasdair could stay in the flat on Marchmont Terrace for the rest of his life. But a big surprise was coming. I actually knew about something that Alasdair didn't. Morag had shown me her will and I knew that there would be a pretty large sum of money coming Alasdair's way. He was totally amazed. Some of it stayed with him, some of it he gave away. Visiting representatives of some non-existent charities would get a wee cheque.

PART THREE

The fall

It was June 2015, just over a year after Morag's death. So Alasdair was living alone in the Marchmont Terrace flat and he was probably drinking a bit more than he normally would, because he couldn't really do without drinking. He was a functioning alcoholic, he would have been the first to admit that, so I'm not speaking out of turn. This day had been the day of Colin Beattie's dad's funeral. And Alasdair and Robert went to the purvey at the Òran Mór after the funeral, and there was a lot to drink. And Robert left, I think about 6ish or something, but Alasdair stayed on, and Robert still feels very guilty about this. He wishes he'd stayed behind to make sure Alasdair got home safely, but he didn't because, well, Alasdair's a grown man. Everybody wanted to talk to Alasdair and he was being given a lot to drink and he really enjoyed talking to people and telling stories. He was in his element. Eventually, after far far too much to drink, he got himself home. Somehow.

Where's the steps? Where's the door?

Here's the door. I went to put my key in the door. Fell backwards, May.

That's what I remember, May.

Stupid bugger, Gray.

Then I went forward again, got the key in and must have lost my footing, May.

Think I put my hand out for the railing, May.

Did try.

Did.

Don't remember.

The railings at the side of the front steps are not very high. A little below waist height. Fine ornate Victorian wrought-iron railings, high enough to stop a toddler, but not a rolling drunk. It's at least an eighteen foot drop from the top of the railing to the concrete of the basement area. He landed on his back and fractured his skull and broke his back.

Still conscious. What was going through his mind? Is this the abyss? What level of hell? Am I dreaming about my Dante book? On the hard hard ground in the rain. Alan, Alan Fletcher, did you go through this too?

Now this was late at night and it was very dark. The Terrace is one side of the little road only; the opposite side all high trees and thick bushes. There was nobody around to see him, nobody to hear anything. How long did he lie there? Down below street level. Nobody can tell. They couldn't tell. An hour? Two hours?

Finally some neighbours, who lived in the basement flat one along, heard moaning and whimpering and they didn't know what it was. But they knew it was human noises they were hearing as the sounds slowly woke them out of their sleep. They were quite frightened. They opened their basement window and climbed out and saw this body lying there. And called an ambulance. Alasdair was both hypothermic and really quite seriously injured when he was admitted to hospital.

But where was I? Alasdair, my love, where was I? Alasdair, my impossible love! Old bugger-lugs, why couldn't I stop you falling? I was in Liverpool, visiting my sister, and I got a call the day after, because everyone knew that I was very close to Alasdair. I got a call from Robert to say Alasdair had had a really bad accident. He's broken his back, they don't know if he'll make it. I was in tears. That's what was said to me, they don't know if he'll make it, and I just came home straightaway.

And then I found out he was in Intensive Care in the Royal Infirmary. Robert had been able to get in to see him and told me that he thought he was going to die.

Intensive care

I rushed to the Royal Infirmary, that turreted brown Victorian pile in old Glasgow by cemetery and cathedral. This was urgent so I got a taxi. Down the hill that Alasdair described as one side of the valley with Byres Road at the bottom, along Great Western Road, onto the M8, off at Townhead, past the Provand's Lordship, down John Knox Street and round the back of the Royal and into the hospital, rushing, half running, my pulse pounding in my ears, desperate to see Alasdair. Would he live? What I had been told was not good. Broken back and fractured skull, hypothermia. Oh Alasdair, Alasdair. You fool, you stupid old fool. I'm coming to see you. I'm on my way. There soon. Don't die.

Down a maze of endless corridors to the Intensive Care Unit in the glass and concrete extensions out the back. Directions incomprehensible. Bloody signs no use. Ask a porter. Ask a receptionist. At last. Here's the door. Big solid locked door. Of course, it's locked. It's Intensive Care. Can't just wander in. Have to be admitted as a special visitor. At last. Made it. Press the buzzer. Here comes the nurse.

"I'm here to see Alasdair Gray."

"Who are you?"

"I'm his friend, May."

"Do you have the code?"

"Code? What code? Nobody's given me a code."

"Sorry, you're not allowed in without a code. His son has contacted us and said anyone visiting needs to have a code to get into the ward to visit because he's quite a well-known person."

"He's not that well-known!" He wasn't – not like a rock star or royalty, he was just known to those in the literary and art scene.

"I don't know what you're talking about. I've come rushing here to visit. I need to see Alasdair. He's my friend. He's a very important person to me!"

"Sorry but you must have the code. It has to be his son's way of looking after him. He must be very special to him."

She wouldn't let me in. I walked away, tears blinding me.

Although Robert had visited the day before, he was now no longer able to visit. And yet Robert worked very closely with Alasdair, he was really close. It was the most impossible nightmarish situation.

So I phoned Stef who at times worked as his secretary.

"I need the code to see Alasdair."

Although Stef and I got on well, he said that he couldn't give me the code.

"Why not?"

"Because Andrew has asked me not to share it."

I was absolutely gobsmacked and couldn't believe it because Alasdair's son, Andrew, who lived in America, as well as his sister, Mora, who lives in Alnwick in Northumberland, knew how close Alasdair and I were. They knew everything I had been doing in supporting him.

I phoned Mora.

"I can't believe this. I don't understand, Mora – could you please sort this out?"

Anyway, she couldn't sort it out. Mora is a nice woman, but wouldn't go against Andrew's wishes.

"Do you have the code, Mora?"

"I do. Andrew gave it to me. But I can't give it to you."

"When are you next in Glasgow?"

"I'll be there tomorrow afternoon."

"Can I come with you and visit him? I'm actually really upset."

I was really upset, and she understood, but her hands were tied.

So I ended up going to the hospital with Mora when she came through to Glasgow – and I could only ever visit him in the Royal when she was there too.

And when I first saw him I just welled up, he was in an induced coma with an endotracheal tube in his mouth attached to a ventilator. His urinary bag was hanging out of the bed. All I could hear was the low hum of the ventilator. Keeping him alive. His colour was poor and I really thought there was a good chance that he wasn't going to make it. But this was Alasdair. He'd come back from a heart attack.

While Mora was in Glasgow I asked her for the code a few times more, but she couldn't give it to me as Andrew would be angry – saying that she couldn't be disloyal. I was upset; not at all angry with her, it wasn't her fault.

"You're talking about disloyalty, this is terrible! I have always been loyal to Alasdair."

Anyway, I didn't get the code.

Fortunately, Mora visited often and stayed at Alasdair's flat, so that was okay, and I could visit him when she was here.

I was so upset, really; I was beside myself, not understanding.

On my third or fourth visit I took a soft toy, a large red lobster to remind him of Alice in Wonderland and the Lobster Quadrille (Will you walk a little faster?) and although he seemed unconscious I'm sure he squeezed my hand.

++++

Towards the end of August the Royal decided they had to transfer him as he was improving and needed to be in a rehabilitation unit. They transferred him to the Spinal Unit of the Queen Elizabeth University Hospital in Glasgow. Thereafter Andrew, his son, who had arrived in Glasgow at some point without letting me know, went home to America. He seemed to vanish off the face of the earth, I never saw him the whole time he was in Glasgow. I tried to contact him. I knew that he was staying at Alasdair's flat, almost next door to me on Marchmont Terrace. Mora told me. I knocked on the door. I left voicemails on Alasdair's landline answerphone. I put a note through the door. Could you please call me. I want to know how your dad is.

He didn't respond at all. What should I make of that? Am I an evil monster to be avoided? Am I a threat? Do I have the plague?

My contact was always with Mora who was happy for me to take over visiting him in the QEUH Spinal Unit where I didn't need a code.

"Can you make sure he's okay?" said Mora.

And I said, "Of course!"

Mora was lovely and happy for my involvement, suggesting that perhaps I could become involved as I had been before his accident.

Treasure Island

In my head I can still hear that rasping, croaky voice trying to sound like a one-legged pirate with a parrot on his shoulder. No typical patient this.

Alasdair kept on improving and when he was transferred from the Royal Infirmary to the Spinal Unit of the Queen Elizabeth Hospital for rehab, then I could see him. There was no door code or nurse to get past. It was fine to get in at the Spinal Unit because he was getting better and was now compos mentis, no longer on the brink and could say what he wanted and what he didn't, which was great. And he wanted to see me, so I could visit him without interrogation about how did I know him and could I provide the secret code. They had barred me from visiting him when he was thought to be dying, and I doubt I will ever get over it.

On my frequent visits, I could, I thought, sometimes bore him because I had little to say except ask him what they had done that day regarding rehabilitation work and ask how he was feeling and what was he thinking about because Alasdair always had a busy mind. But he was still recovering, unable to speak clearly because the tracheal tube had caused a bit of a vocal issue. Perhaps this needs more explanation. When they removed the tubing, it likely caused irritation and swelling and the normal mucous membrane that keeps vocal folds moist can also become thickened. Alasdair's full bellow never returned, even though his almost normal speaking voice reappeared.

When we spoke, Alasdair's voice seemed sore and scratchy. It was hard for me to hear, and I think, for a while, it hurt to speak. And he was exhausted. He asked if I could read to him. He wanted me to read *Treasure Island* to him, which wasn't a book I loved, albeit like most children in the fifties, I had read it, learned most of it, seen the film and remembered the story.

I especially remember Long John Silver, and also the actors who played the characters in the film, especially Robert Newton as Long John Silver. And I remember the Inn, the Admiral Benbow, where there were all sorts of buccaneers, mad kinds of people, shanghaiing the unsuspecting. And there were different accents and Alasdair not only wanted me to read aloud, but he also wanted me to play the different parts and use the accents of the characters.

And I am crap at accents, and I got embarrassed, and he would say – inasmuch as I could hear him –

"Carry on! Carry on!"

And I would carry on, and he would burst out laughing because my accent sounded more Indian than anything else, Indian gone Welsh, and I think East European. He would burst out laughing, even with his voice not fully recovered, and imitate accents that were barely audible. And he did them well. He had an ear for accents, and boy could he do it.

"Continue! May, continue!" he would say.

And I said, "Oh no!"

And of course, when the nurses came into the ward, they heard what was going on and they found it hilarious. When they were there, they offered tea to the patients and although refreshments were meant for the patients, they were very good and offered me a coffee. I would re-assure them it was okay to laugh at me.

"I'm rubbish at accents, I've never been any good at accents."

Alasdair had broken his back and so sitting on a chair for any length of time caused considerable pain. He had a brace on his back and his skin was excoriated, red and sore. The nurses were wonderful, but it was difficult to prevent the redness. So he liked it best when I read to him in the evening when he was lying down with the back brace removed. I saw when he was in a chair that his leg muscles had almost faded away. His legs were like lit-tle sticks, he didn't weigh a lot, although he looked heavy, it was all belly, and his poor wee legs just couldn't support him, even for transferring from chair to wheelchair.

The care staff would try to stand him up with the use of a hoist, but he had a hard time and hearing him moan made me wince. I loathed seeing him in pain.

When I read to him, it was usually for about an hour or more until my throat got sore, because I had to double back on the voices, trying to get the accent, but failing miserably. But he knew the story better than me, repeating it back softly when I couldn't manage the accents. He could repeat the lines almost verbatim. Alasdair had one of these memories. If he enjoyed a book, he remembered every bit; and he loved *Treasure Island*, absolutely loved it. I remember saying to him, this is funny.

"I think Robert Louis Stevenson was maybe a murderer. I heard that somewhere."

"Don't be silly, that's daft!" Alasdair sharp as a knife.

"No, I'm sure I read that somewhere."

"What, no, you couldn't have?"

"Did I say Robert Louis Stevenson? Oh my god, I meant Arthur Conan Doyle."

And he also loved Conan Doyle, but he hadn't read about these rumours. I apologised and explained they had suspected Conan Doyle of murder, but that the stories weren't credible, simply malicious rumours. He didn't believe me, but given that he knew nothing of these stories, for a change, I was the one conveying information about writers. It felt quite good, as I always felt a little inadequate because I did not have Alasdair's knowledge, especially about writers. Anyway, we had a jolly good laugh about the mix-up and the daft rumour mill.

So I read to him again, telling him it would have been very exciting being in the Admiral Benbow Inn with the Buccaneers.

"Ooh-Aar-Jim-lad!" exclaimed Alasdair.

"Shiver-me-timbers," said I in my best pirate voice. We had great fun when I attempted to read that book. And I finished it before they discharged him home. It was worth the effort because of the laughs we had.

The others in the ward also seemed to enjoy the tale. In the far left corner there was a boy in the bed who couldn't stop laughing. They say laughter is the best medicine.

Getting him home

When Alasdair was in the Spinal Unit, I usually visited in the evening when I knew there would be fewer visitors – and by then the nurses would have propped him up in bed. Although sometimes I also visited him during the day when he was sitting upright in a chair, a time which was often painful for him because of the back support, his brace, cutting into him.

The ward they had admitted him to in the Spinal Unit was a shared space. When I read to him, there were usually only another two people there. It's a rehab unit, so they aim to get people as fit as possible for discharge home, and after that, it's mainly outpatient appointments. But Alasdair couldn't go home, he just couldn't. There wasn't anyone there. He lived alone. His wife Morag died in 2014 and this was the latter part of 2015. There wasn't anyone at home to care for him and he wasn't well enough to go home anyway. His physiotherapy wasn't going well. There were problems with incontinence and often therapy could not proceed or had to be stopped. However, by the time they believed him ready for home, or more or less ready for home, they said, "We need to be thinking of discharging him soon, he's been here a while. He's getting well enough for home. So what's happening at home May, what's going on?"

"But he can't go home on his own. Honestly, nothing is happening at home. Alasdair lives alone and can't go home until we make a plan for adaptations. His home is unsuitable and it's going to need alterations."

I think I was almost in tears by then.

I let Mora know, I always kept her informed. I said I would do my utmost to make sure that he was safe. I also said that I didn't know how I could persuade them to keep him in a unit that they said was no longer appropriate as they'd done as much as they could. This was the NHS and they needed the bed.

I really had to try my hardest, I was so anxious during that time, nobody else seemed interested in how he would get home – and I really do think he would have gone straight into care, a holding place until there was somewhere suitable for him to go, but nothing was happening. I phoned Mora back.

"I'm going to organise a home care meeting if it's okay with the family."

"Oh yes, that's fine!"

I had the family's agreement.

There were about three home care meetings, with doctors, physiotherapists, occupational therapists and the discharge team. I attended all of them. And with some difficulty I got them to delay discharge. Samantha, his recent secretary, came to one of the meetings. The hospital staff asked me who I was, was I family?

"His son lives in Connecticut and his sister is in England. But I have Alasdair's permission to act on his behalf."

"Is that true, Alasdair?"

"Certainly. Of course she has. May needs to know everything necessary to get me home."

I listed what he needed.

"The bathroom door is tiny, very tiny and a wheelchair would never fit – and he only has a small bath which is squished in. They made the space for the bathroom in a converted part of a terraced townhouse – it's a kind of cupboard size and there is no shower, and a shower wouldn't fit unless over the bath – and he can't walk. How would he manage? A wet room will be necessary as Alasdair doesn't have use of his legs and also his arms and hands seem weakened. There seems to be little strength there. I have observed him trying to transfer. His arms don't have the strength to support his body from chair to bed. He can't get himself into his wheelchair."

So I said I would try to arrange builders, but I would need planning permission. I was pretty stressed. They wanted him to leave, but they assured him they would make efforts to prolong his stay in the hospital for a little while, as they had completed his hospital care. And could I plan for him to go home within six weeks.

Conversation in October 2015, going into November. I was worried.

I spoke with Alasdair to tell him what needed to be done for him to get home and that the medical staff had said that six weeks was as long as they could keep him.

I said I would do my best, but didn't know if we could do the adaptations within six weeks.

"Alasdair, for you to go home, we need to completely re-configure your bathroom. A wall will need to be knocked through to your bedroom to make a wide enough space for the wheelchair."

He instructed me to do whatever it took. I had his permission. He was upset that he could not manage as before and that the flat he loved would need to be altered. I reassured him that yes I would do whatever it took to get the work done.

That was when I asked around, speaking to friends to get recommendations.

I managed, after a time, to get plans drawn up, plans that he didn't particularly agree with at first. He wanted to see other plans. How this was to be paid for hadn't then occurred to him. I understood he was ill and desperate to get home to his beloved West End flat and I didn't push the issue.

He was quite optimistic, and I thought that was a good thing. He also thought that by the time six weeks had passed, he could likely walk again. Although unrealistic, it was, I thought, good for him to have such hope; it kept him going. But sadly, there was little chance of that happening.

The hospital staff thought he might get more strength in one leg than the other, but he couldn't bear his weight with his arms. He'd lost muscle tone. And strength. I thought and so did they, even though it wasn't said, that he would never walk again. And he never did, and that was so sad. And Alasdair tried, he tried and tried, but he simply couldn't. It was awful.

When I consulted with him again about the adaptations, he again debated with me. He didn't think that knocking a part of a wall down was a good idea, annoyed that it would ruin his bedroom wall, where he hung his many paintings.

"Well, sadly, it's that or they may want to transfer you to a facility in the meantime while we figure out something else, and I don't know what other options we have."

I was calm and sympathetic when discussing the issue, holding his hand because it was his home and he'd had such a dreadful accident and his resulting disability had traumatised him enough. I understood, but the NHS wanted the bed. Unfortunately the NHS is not a long-term facility.

"No, no, no, I am going to my home!" he exclaimed as loudly as his voice allowed him.

"I am doing the best I can, Alasdair. So can you agree with these plans? Tell me what you think?" I showed him the architectural drawings again and, although understandably upset rationally, he knew he couldn't go home unless the flat was adapted.

"Okay, okay, okay, you get it done."

He wasn't happy about it. It was his home, the place he lived in, and they were going to knock down a main wall. I suggested I could reposition the paintings. The ceilings were high and I could rehang them. He shrugged resignedly.

"OK, that's okay, that's what we'll do."

I said that I hadn't yet costed it, but I pushed it no further. I didn't want to burden him with more worrying information.

It was to cost around £6000 to knock down the wall, repair the area and fit the wet room, but I can't remember the exact figure.

I had to have planning permission. I was lucky in that I've got friends who helped me contact Glasgow City Council Planning quickly and also helped to draw up plans. We were fortunate to have such genuine friends. They also said because it was Alasdair they would waive the fee.

I was given a recommendation and engaged builders. I didn't have a choice; I was on a deadline. I knew nothing about building or building regulations and had to rely on the goodwill of my friends.

The work began. I was so scared because all the paintings were still on the walls and some propped up along the skirtings, everywhere actually. I took some down from the wall area that was to be demolished and covered them with sheets and whatever protective material I could find. I also bought large sheets of plastic, and the builders also brought along protective materials. The workers were very good and didn't mind me popping in daily to see how they were getting along. They knocked the wall through, made the wet room and made a new wide wheelchair-accessible door, built into the space. And the paintings were unharmed. It was a good job, not the high spec I would have wanted, but it was the best we could afford.

I wept when I saw it because I knew he could now get home. All that remained to be done was to make a home care plan and organise further aids and a hospital-style bed to go to his flat.

Alasdair, to me, was always hard-up for money and I don't think even he knew what he had in the bank. He was trying so hard to get well enough to go home, but the reality was the builders had to be paid. I'd already contacted friends and asked again. These were friends who admired him very much and some seemed pretty well off, but when I asked, only one person offered money to help and that was Alasdair's friend George, the organiser of the Jolly Boys, and I will always be grateful to him. Always a bright light in a dark corner, George.

I reluctantly told Alasdair, "We're going to have a shortfall of about three thousand pounds. What are we going to do, Alasdair? We need to do this. I can probably pay it, but I have little disposable income, but can likely get a loan easily."

He began laughing. "Oh, no you won't, I'll write you a cheque May, but I don't have my chequebook."

I nervously said, "Do you have enough?" He said that he didn't know but thought so. He was always a bit vague about matters financial. I again said that if this didn't work out, I would pay it somehow.

He told me where I could find his chequebook. I always had keys for Alasdair's, and he had keys for my flat, just in case anything ever happened.

But oh oh oh

oh oh oh oh oh oh

oh oh the pain.

OMG me in QEUH too

The ambulance came to collect me from my flat in Marchmont Terrace and took me to the Queen Elizabeth University Hospital. I couldn't move my head. Or my right arm. I was terrified, thought I was going to die. The bones in my upper cervical spine were compressing the nerves. And the pain was unbearable.

I was admitted to the QEUH for pain control and was to spend 9 days in hospital being given drugs to make the pain bearable. More or less bearable. Surgery was going to be needed at a later date. But light-headed as I was with all this medication, organising Alasdair's home support had to carry on. Couldn't stop now. In the second week of this stay, I was able to make phonecalls to all concerned.

Then one evening in the middle of my hospital stay the door opened and there was the nurse.

"I've got someone here to see you."

And Alasdair was wheeled in by the nurse from the Spinal Unit. A big beam on his face.

"I'll be back for you, Alasdair." The nurse left. Having got a nurse to wheel him all the way, and it was a long way,

from the Spinal Unit to my ward was a major achieve-
ment. He must have sweet-talked the nurse.

"Goodness May, what are you doing here! Robert told
me you were in. I'm so so so happy to see you. This is the
perfect exercise in the tragi-comic."

I was in pain and still so delighted to see him. We
talked for some 40 minutes, this other focus helping to
take my mind off the pain. But finally, it was too much of
an effort to concentrate, rising above the medication too
much to do.

"I'll be back, May. See you again."

We tried to hug but with me in my bed and him in his
wheelchair it didn't work.

Home we go

I took the chequebook to him and he wrote the cheque and I didn't ask him about it, just grateful that I could pay the builders.

Unfortunately, he made the cheque out to me, not the builders, which I was uncomfortable with, but that was Alasdair. He trusted me to pay the builders. I think he wanted to know who exactly was getting the money; it was sometimes hard to read Alasdair and how his mind worked.

So I had to pay the cheque into my account (Alasdair's cheque didn't bounce) and then settle with the builders. We paid the builders and, of course, we used George's money. I don't know what I would have done without the support of such good friends. All receipts went to Alasdair.

Time was moving fast toward Christmas and Alasdair was becoming anxious because there was still more work being done to make his flat ready for him. And he was shaky. I visited him on Christmas Eve 2015. He sounded concerned.

"What's happening May? I need to go home."

"We're getting there. We're almost there and Robert's going to paint your bedroom once we have the plastering done."

I told the medical staff too that we were almost there, and they seemed relieved. At the final discharge planning meeting the home care team became involved and all those present asked for a date when Alasdair could be discharged. I would let them all know as soon as I knew, as soon as his flat was ready for him.

And we finished the work on his flat just before Hogmanay. I thought rather than call him at the hospital, I would go visit him on Hogmanay, which I did, and we had a lovely time when I read more of *Treasure Island*; that's when I actually finished the story, much to my relief. When I got home, Robert told me that he had taken a phonecall saying that the work had passed inspection.

So on the first of January, New Year's Day 2016, I phoned my friend, Janet Robertson, because, like Alasdair, I am a Glasgow pedestrian in that I don't drive. Janet knew how important Alasdair was in my life and drove me back to the hospital.

When I arrived, he was all smiles and happy to see me. I said, "All the work is done and we've just heard that it has passed inspection. Alasdair, it's all been okayed. You can go home."

He was so happy that going home was organised.
He asked for a selfie to prove he was alive
(there had been rumours).

He smiled like the Cheshire cat. And tears ran down his face. And mine as I hugged him. I spoke to the nursing staff. There were no doctors around that day.

"I would be grateful if you could let the doctors know to begin the discharge plan."

I'd been to several home planning meetings, so everyone involved knew what had to be in place. Soon after, we started doing just that.

We made plans for him to go home, got everything in place – and home he went!

And from that time to this day I have never heard from his son. Would he have objected to his dad going into care? Which Alasdair would have hated, absolutely hated. I don't know, but I do know that the Dante trilogy would never have been written.

Some time later I told Alasdair to go and say thank you to the basement couple who had found him and almost certainly saved his life. But he never did say thank you to them. I did it for him.

PART FOUR

Back home

Two Glasgow City Council carers came in four times a day to start with, then three times a day. I had wanted an overnight carer too, but that wasn't possible. He could always call me. A dubious thought perhaps… Would he always be able to?

I had a joiner fit a key safe box outside the front door of Number 2. Alasdair and I made up a code between us and I set the code. I also wrote it on a piece of paper for Alasdair. With hindsight, I am unsure if this was a good idea. The home care team and those who needed it received the code. Family who visited had keys, but I also gave them the door code.

The social care team put Alasdair to bed in the evening, assisted him getting out of bed in the morning, heated up whatever food had been brought in or left sandwiches, wheeled him to the toilet, showered him and did everything they could to make him comfortable in the short space of time they had.

The length of the time allocated per client puts considerable pressure on the council care staff, so they would usually put Alasdair to bed around seven-ish after having helped him change into his nightwear and transferring from his wheelchair to bed. Sometime later we were able to ask that they make Alasdair their last visit of the evening if something important was to be arranged – such as Alasdair going out to a Jolly Boys session or if he was giving a reading. But even at that, it couldn't be too late.

His housekeeper Florence was also reemployed during the day.

My own life was nothing if not busy around this time, when Alasdair was now back home at Marchmont Terrace. I was juggling two roles in the later years of my career. Although teaching social work practice at Glasgow Caledonian University had now finished, I was now a part-time social work practice teacher and a part-time tutor in social work at the University of Strathclyde (two part-times make more than one full-time). I had the notion that the future of the NHS could be changed through a focus on improved social work. Not infrequently I would be called away from work, say when I was grading papers, because of an emergency with Alasdair back at Marchmont Terrace.

One of the first things Alasdair did after being discharged from the Spinal Unit was to go out and crash a funeral, or more accurately to crash the reception after the funeral. Well, maybe 'crash' is not quite the word. The writer William McIlvanney had died in December 2015 but a remembrance service was to be held some months later, in April 2016, in Glasgow University's Bute Hall and Alasdair absolutely had to be there. He hadn't been invited, not so much probably because he wouldn't be welcome but rather because there was general uncertainty about his ability to get about. And was he even still alive? His friend, George Tomlinson, took him along to the Bute Hall and wheeled him in. But the two of them didn't know exactly where to go and accidentally stumbled into the sad family mourners' room, where about a dozen people had gathered. George apologises and starts to push Alasdair back out, but the family were so delighted to see Alasdair that they greeted him and George with open arms and gave Alasdair a hero's welcome. A little levity in the sombre occasion.

Some months later Andrew gave his old friend Gary the job of additional carer with the idea of giving Alasdair some physiotherapy. I myself wouldn't have thought that a foot pedal exerciser was going to work for Alasdair; and was Alasdair ever going to be capable of shaving himself? Wasn't it too risky for him to even try?

Cut himself? Chest infection? Here we were again. And again and again and again. Back in the ambulance back to the hospital. Me taking Alasdair to hospital again. Between the time of his return home and his final days, during those four years, he was in and out of hospital I don't know how many times. I think many of these trips could have been avoided. We needed a new care arrangement, we really did. Each time he was going back to the same problematic environment. With no night care. I expressed my concerns to the family several times. I knew Alasdair well enough to understand that he would never ask for help himself.

The cut and the book

This was the second time I'd taken him to hospital after he'd cut himself shaving – nicking an artery. I had tried to stop the bleeding but only had small hemostatic dressings in my first aid kit – and after 20 minutes stopping the bleed proved impossible. I had to call an ambulance. Even at the hospital it took the doctors about a half hour with more appropriate hemo-static dressings etc and the use of considerable pressure to stem the flow.

He had insisted I get him a book from his home whilst he was being bundled into the ambulance. He needed me to run back inside to get it. I did so reluctantly.

We had a bit of a tiff when I told him that he was putting himself at risk should he fall asleep and the book would likely fall on his face and reopen the cut. But he wouldn't listen to me. But he also knew that, should he become sleepy, I would remove the book. And he did. And I did.

He could be very stubborn at times. No matter where we went, a book was always there.

Florence

And it goes without saying that Florence, dear Florence, got the code. She also had a set of keys.

In the story of Alasdair's journey back home, the role of Florence, his housekeeper, is crucial. Morag had hired Florence to carry out household duties when she fell ill, which began her connection to Alasdair and Florence's commitment continued after Morag died.

Picture Florence: a petite, tidy woman with short, dark hair from the Wyndford, a council estate in Maryhill, and a smile you could readily trust. Florence was the salt of the earth, no airs and graces, what you saw was what you got. She was an angel, a godsend.

After Alasdair's discharge from the QEUH, Florence seamlessly resumed the housekeeping role and worked harmoniously with the home care team. While not formally a caregiver, Florence went way beyond her job description, infusing her role with compassion. It was not her job to take him to the toilet, but she would do it.

Colin Beattie stepped in with meals from the Òran Mór, identifying nutritional needs post-hospitalisation.

Florence also recognised the significance of the meals and ensured their delivery. She also collected them to lighten the load on the staff at the Òran Mór, going out of her way because she saw what was needed. Florence, ever humble, admitted she wasn't much of a cook, but ensured that Alasdair had enough to eat, either serving it herself or leaving it for the home care team to heat if he wasn't hungry when she left. The Ubiquitous Chip also offered to make a daily food delivery, but Alasdair didn't take this up, although he clearly appreciated the offer.

Florence already knew about Alasdair's excessive drinking. Morag and Alasdair were self-confessed alcoholics. Despite this, she respected his autonomy as an adult. Although she believed he was trying to control his drinking, she realised he couldn't physically pour drinks, so she kindly motivated him to cut back while at the same time making sure there was always a drink next to him on his bedside table, as he'd asked.

Florence and I were in constant communication about Alasdair and she regularly checked in with me to let me know how he was doing.

Bump in the night

Alasdair was insistent that everything he needed should be on his bed table, the little table that sat across the bed, because he had cot-sides on his bed to prevent him from rolling over and falling out of bed. He would have all his important paraphernalia, his pens, ink, books and paper, on this table.

On one night, and I think it was soon after his return home, it wasn't more than the second week, he dropped a pen and another important item from the bed and stretched over to get it. Now I do not know what happened earlier in the evening, but I do know that the carers always put the cot-sides back in place. However, if Alasdair had a visitor, he might have been more comfortable asking that the cot-side be down, and the visitor might have left without remembering or indeed being reminded to put the side back up in position. This had potentially disastrous consequences.

This night on reaching and reaching and reaching to retrieve the item, he stretched out too far and toppled out of bed, thumping hard down onto the wooden floorboards. He lay there whimpering. I knew nothing of this.

There was no one employed during the night to see to his needs. The care package didn't include night care, which was virtually impossible to get.

His neighbour downstairs had heard a thump and I got a telephone call.

"May, I think something has happened to Alasdair. I heard a thump on the floor."

"Oh for feck's sake! Oh my God!"

"I've called 999, but could you see if he is alright?"

"I'm putting on my dressing gown. I'll be right down!"

She knew I had keys (I always had keys, even when Morag was alive, because of possible difficulties). I jumped out of bed into my slippers and wrapped my dressing-gown around me. I must've looked a sight running along Marchmont Terrace with bed hair sticking out like the wicked witch of the Terrace. This was around 1.00am.

I got into the flat and, just as I arrived, so did the police and then the paramedics. I was attempting to lift him but realised I couldn't do it. Alasdair was lying there looking completely helpless and wretched. I immediately felt a hard lump in my throat, which I suppressed not wanting to distress Alasdair further. It was so upsetting. The paramedics took charge and assessed him to confirm that he had not sustained any injuries or broken any bones.

They were wonderful. They picked him up, settled him back into bed, tucked him in, gave him a glass of water and checked his catheter to ensure it hadn't been pulled out or become entangled in the fall, making sure he was okay. They were so good. The police were brilliant too.

"What is a vulnerable man like this doing on his own at night?" the police asked. They clearly weren't happy about the situation they had been called out to.

"I know, I know, it's a problem, I have tried," I said. I think they thought I was his daughter. And I was even starting to feel guilty, apologising for something I couldn't control.

The emergency services were making some light-hearted banter with Alasdair, knowing how embarrassed he was. But they also gave him a serious warning about keeping safe during the night. I had a chat with the emergency services too and apologised to them as well, although it had nothing to do with me. I still felt guilty that they needed to be called.

When they all left, I stayed behind and had a quiet word with Alasdair.

"Alasdair you can't do that. You almost gave me a heart attack. I'm so bloody grateful to your neighbour for phoning me, she couldn't have known when the paramedics would arrive."

I said that he owed her a bunch of flowers or a box of chocolates. I am not sure if she ever got them.

I was still a bit stunned and upset and I tried to tell him as kindly as I could because he'd already been to hell after his terrible fall and I didn't want to cause further distress. But I had to tell him off.

"Please never do that again. Alasdair, please make sure that if the cot-sides are taken down for any reason, you ask to have them put back in place because you are so vulnerable during the night. I bloody hate speaking to you like this. I don't want to treat you like a toddler, but you really can't do that again. These cot-sides cannot be down when you're on your own. It's only human nature to stretch out for something. My god, you could have killed yourself! If you want to stay at home you have to stay safe. Neither of us want you to be in a care home. The cot-sides are back up now and they are staying like that until you're in your wheelchair in the morning! Promise me you won't do this again."

"I promise not to do it again, May," he said rather sheepishly.

I sat with him for a while and we had a long chat. I changed the subject and we talked about other things, other more interesting things, until he became drowsy and then I left. I was emotionally exhausted.

"You've been gone about an hour and a half," said Robert.

"I know, I know. I was just making sure everything was okay."

Joyce Gunn Cairns
comes to visit

Joyce Gunn Cairns, an artist from Edinburgh, had read *Poor Things* and absolutely loved it.

She knew also that Alasdair lived next door to her ex's twin sister, so Joyce had often visited Marchmont Terrace. Joyce had written to Alasdair asking if he would mind if she tried to draw him and he agreed.

Joyce clearly remembers the first time she ever visited. Alasdair opened the door and had her laughing before she even stepped inside. Joyce found him as easy to be with as did I. Never any airs and graces, so conversation was never a problem. It was during that first visit he suggested they exhibit together, which thrilled Joyce. And they did it several times, initially in the Smithy Gallery in Blanefield, and then in the Sutton and the Union galleries in Edinburgh. By the time of the last two exhibitions, Alasdair had had his terrible accident.

Joyce had come through several times to draw him before his disabling fall.

The last time Joyce visited I was there too. Alasdair was then in a wheelchair. She was keen to come through to Glasgow to see him and Alasdair told me that perhaps they might discuss future events. Alasdair was delighted, looking forward to the visit. He liked Joyce. These were always happy occasions.

Alasdair asked if I could help because he wanted to give Joyce lunch and knew they wouldn't be able to go out for lunch unless someone took him in the wheelchair. He also wanted a friendly informal lunch which would be better managed in his own home where he was comfortable.

I said he shouldn't worry at all, and that it would make me happy to cook for him so he could entertain Joyce at home. I suggested we get out the wee table and set it up. Florence helped me set the table up. Florence was a treasure. I also asked if she would like to stay for something to eat, but she declined. I think she was a little shy about being involved in the lunch.

So the table was set for the three of us. Joyce arrived, and I suggested they might want to eat together to discuss potential plans in private, but both Joyce and Alasdair insisted I stay. So I stayed.

It was awkward trying to manoeuvre Alasdair's chair so that he could sit comfortably at the wee table as the wheelchair easily got caught in the legs of the table, but

I successfully manoeuvred it in, and it was a joy to see him happy to have a visitor he was so looking forward to seeing.

I made mince and tatties, just very plain ordinary good solid Scottish fare, mainly because Alasdair liked that type of food and also loved my cooking. I suspected not much could go wrong, and I served it up, and the three of us had a great old blether. To enable the pair to discuss any projects I frequently left the room, clearing away plates and getting drinks.

I became friendly with Joyce and we would email each other. When Alasdair became very unwell, I also phoned her to let her know he was dying. I knew how fond she was of him and he of her.

Clydebuilt

Later in 2016, after Alasdair's discharge home, the searing pain I'd been experiencing in my neck and right arm became relentless. It was unbearable. I took a staggering amount of medication prescribed by the doctors to suppress the pain, but these drugs left my mind clouded in a disorienting fog. They also failed to numb the agony, causing me to become a bewildered shadow person. Yet I knew I had to, as they say, soldier on, gritting my teeth to continue daily activities.

But I couldn't endure my chemical prison much longer. The pain had become a waking nightmare and the medications unsatisfying sedation, and I honestly had a genuine fear of addiction. I had no choice. Surgery had become inevitable.

I mentally prepared myself, letting my family and Alasdair know. I told Alasdair I couldn't help with heavy lifting for a minimum of 6 weeks post-surgery.

Explaining this to Alasdair filled me with guilt. I worried he might need help during the night and I couldn't be present. But Robert, ever dependable, allayed my fears, volunteering his services should the need arise.

Alasdair's face betrayed his alarm when I told him I needed surgery. I sensed he was feeling guilty because I was feeling guilty, though he did not deserve this burden.

As the date for the surgery drew closer, I found my mind overwhelmed with concerns about Alasdair.

"Please don't worry, May. I'll be fine," he assured me, his words offering cold comfort. Anxiety twisted me.

At last, the Queen Elizabeth Hospital, or as it is known locally, the Death Star, admitted me for my ACDF – the Anterior Cervical Discectomy with Fusion – a strange-sounding, major surgical procedure to relieve the nerve compression in my neck that tortured me. I clung to my coping mechanism of dubbing it ACDC after the famed band, not the electrical system, desperately seeking levity wherever I could find it. In reality, fear gripped me, remembering previous spinal surgery to decompress my lumbar region – a harrowing ordeal I didn't wish to relive. But I concealed my fears and put on my bravest face.

The surgeon was excellent and skilfully performed the ACDF, but afterwards I went through several days of agonising silence when my voice deserted me.

My friends slowly arrived to cheer me up. My sister brought me ice pops to relieve my sore throat. I have never enjoyed ice lollies as much as I did then – like a gift from the gods, truly divine!

Robert's unexpected arrival with Alasdair surprised me. Seeing them made me happy. Although Alasdair greeted me warmly, he couldn't hide his morbid curiosity about what exactly they had done to me.

So I entertained him by sharing the grisly details of precisely what surgical marvels the doctors had performed on my spine. I slowly, because my voice was croaky, told him how they'd implanted a titanium plate and screws to fuse the vertebrae so as to free the nerve impingement. Both mesmerised and troubled, Alasdair studied the photographs on my iPhone depicting ACDF work similar to the surgery performed on my cervical spine.

"My god, May – you're Clydebuilt!"

I laughed as hard as my fractured voice allowed. Strange to hear these words from the man who had so vividly, viscerally chronicled anatomy, physiology and the reanimation of Bella Baxter in *Poor Things* – yet here he was, gaping in wonder at the comparatively ordinary capabilities of modern surgery.

"Alasdair, for someone who can compose such florid accounts of morbid anatomy and the reanimation of the dead, you seem well able to compartmentalise your writing from reality."

I was thankful for our shared sense of humour as we laughed. This laughter helped in the healing process and eased my conscience.

Inky night

On a memorable night Alasdair called me from his landline. He did not have a mobile phone and would never consider having one. I once asked him if he thought mobile phones caused brain cancer. That was not the reason!

"May, I've had a bit of a spill with the ink," he confessed, his voice laced with a mixture of distress and self-deprecation.

"I'll be right down." It was after midnight and another twist in our friendship was coming up.

So I armed myself with baby wipes and a gentle soap cleanser for sensitive skin, knowing that this would likely be a bit of a clean-up job and that Alasdair had sensitive skin.

I arrived to find Alasdair in a sticky situation with Quink ink, his trusted medium for line drawings, accidentally spilt. Poor Alasdair was lying in bed there with ink-covered hands.

There was also some ink on the front of his nightshirt, on his beard, ink everywhere. I removed the top covers quickly and covered him with a big bath towel

I'd brought with me until I could clean him up and re-make the bed. The bottom sheet wasn't too bad as most of the ink had spilt on the top cover, and it wasn't a full bottle, thankfully. Alasdair was keen for me to help and although I couldn't remove the ink completely, I managed most of it.

I tried to make the entire process light-hearted, laughing and engaging him by saying "What are you like?" and he laughed back. We discussed what he had been doing, and he told me about his work. I spoke while I gently scrubbed him down, not too roughly because of his eczema. I had the basin of water perched on the wee over-the-bed table that I had moved to sit alongside the bed to help me.

As I gently washed his hands, we spoke of how he was managing with everyday life and how I was managing with mine.

I knew that he would need a change of nightshirt and clean bedding, which was to hand because Florence was a brilliant housekeeper and always had everything folded away neatly.

So I changed the bedcovers as best I could, keeping up the cot-sides as I pumped up the bed to waist height and asked that he cross his arms over his chest and checked that he had done so as best he could. Once safely on his side and with a pillow to protect him from the bed rails,

I was going to roll the clean sheet onto the middle of the bed then gently roll him back onto it and repeat the action from the other side, making sure the opposite bed rail was in the raised position for protection. Alasdair was laughing about all this. And so was I.

"Up on one side, Alasdair, ready... go."

"Ooomph."

"Inky sheet coming out."

"OK."

"Fresh sheet coming in."

"Good."

"Need to push this under your bottom. I hope this isn't embarrassing you."

"I AM NOT EMBARRASSED ABOUT ANYTHING NOW!"

"Right, rolling you over now."

"Is that you done?"

"I'm not very used to doing this type of bedroom manoeuvre alone."

"You certainly do know how to make a man feel good in bed, May."

Changing his bedding took a while, and I told him the entire process would have been easier if we'd used Swarfega or an industrial solvent. We both laughed hard. It was so good to hear him laugh like that. It had been a while.

Anyway, I got most of the ink off. Both of us settled down to a nice cuppa (well Alasdair had an Irish coffee). I thought this would ease the distress he must've experienced. He looked very chuffed with himself, smiling despite the ordeal.

I knew that if the sheets became untucked during the night, as soon as the carers arrived in the morning, they would get him up for a shower and remake or change his bed. So I kissed him gently on the head and gave him his books. I left an ink pen and some paper. I believe it was a Rotring fine liner, not the Quink and nib pen! I said jokingly why I was leaving the liner as I couldn't trust him with the Quink! The man needed to keep his brain engaged if unable to sleep!

I took the inky sheets home to soak for several days. I told Florence that I had the sheets just in case she wondered where they'd gone.

Alasdair knew he could reach out to me at any time, even in the darkest hours of the night when he was upset, and I would always be there to listen. Sometimes, I would even go to him. As time passed, he grew increasingly vulnerable, particularly during the late hours of the night. Eventually, I documented my worries in a detailed report and sent it to Mora and Katrina, her daughter, in December 2019, detailing the risks of the absence of totally integrated care and stressing that, since the present care arrangement was not proving satisfactory, with Alasdair going in and out of hospital, a completely fresh care arrangement was required. But by the time I did this it was too late.

More Jolly Boys

There was to be another Jolly Boys session, that drinking club of some twenty men. And Alasdair had missed a few after his fall and he was keen to get back in the swing. And the Jolly Boys were certainly keen to have Alasdair back among them again and George Tomlinson, the organiser and good friend of Alasdair, didn't have any problem at all in getting Alasdair to agree to come along. These were decent men and they really enjoyed their day, all the more so when Alasdair was there. Alasdair could tell stories; he was a good spinner of yarns, and he was in his element in that sort of company with the drinks flowing. Only now, after the fall, his voice projection was not what it had been. There was one cardinal Jolly Boys rule: men only, no women allowed.

After his accident Alasdair couldn't walk. He could get about only by using a wheelchair and that's where I came in. But I am a woman.

Another jolly had been organised. It was to be held in the Òran Mór, and Alasdair absolutely had to get there. He was invited and he simply couldn't miss it. No way.

But not so straightforward. Wheeling him downhill from his flat to the Òran Mór wasn't easy. But that was my job and I did it, solo this time.

George, the organiser, one of your typical west of Scotland quite sexist chaps, but who I liked a lot, laughed, delighted to see Alasdair being wheeled in.

"You know that you have to go now, May – boys only!"

Alasdair wanted me there, but I understood the concept, although Alasdair didn't approve. I was reluctant to leave him – I knew Alasdair would need me to take him discreetly to the loo to empty his urinary leg bag. This was not something he could do by himself. They would drink, and the bag would soon fill up.

"You have to go!" said George again, good-naturedly.

I had to make a point, discreetly but firmly.

"George, I can't go anywhere. Alasdair has a catheter, and you'll be drinking all afternoon. Nobody here will think of emptying the bag, nor do I think you know how."

I said I was worried about the possibility of it being too full, and if he somehow got a backflow, it could result in a urinary infection. There was also the risk of the catheter line getting tangled up with the wheelchair. This was something that often happened.

"So I'll have to stay here to make sure it's emptied."

George frowned. This was a conflict he hadn't antici-
pated. Could he break club rules?

"Oh no, we can't have you here. This is just for the boys,
it's tradition, you understand."

And I understood, but this wasn't a usual situation, it
wasn't like before when Alasdair was hale and hearty.

"You are one big bugger," I said. And laughed.

I honestly don't mind men-only get-togethers, it's
fine, but this was a needs issue and Alasdair wanted me
to stay. And I did try to stay, but it became uncomfortable. Really blue jokes were being told, some really really
obnoxious, and I'm not sure Alasdair liked them either.
These were pretty decent men, so I think they might've
done it deliberately to get me to shoo. I would have gone
anyway.

So I went. I said that I would be back and forth to make
sure Alasdair was okay. Alasdair gave me a hug as did the
big bugger organiser.

I went for a coffee and came back after an hour and
whispered to Alasdair, after discreetly feeling the bag on
his leg under the table and it was full (it generally was
after several drinks).

"Do you want to go to the loo?"

"Yes," he said, making light of it.

I wheeled him away, emptied his bag, poured the contents into the jug I had brought with me, flushed it down

Robert taking Alasdair home

the loo, got him all cleaned up, made sure there was no discomfort and chatted to keep things light while I washed my hands. He was apologetic that I couldn't stay. I told him I understood.

"Thank you May."

"I'll come back in about an hour." I took him to the table and left. It was hard for me to hang around the area and not be included, not that I wanted to be included, but I worried about him, so I didn't go far.

Since these times I have spoken with George about how things were difficult for me then. He understood and said how sorry he was. He was good to Alasdair, and I like him very much.

The Jolly Boys had great admiration for Alasdair's work but didn't seem to appreciate that since the terrible accident Alasdair also had medical and care needs and couldn't drink for hours on end as before without me or somebody else to make sure he was okay. I doubt that would have ever crossed their minds.

Anyway, on these days, I would ultimately go back for him when it was time to go home. I'd wheel him all the way uphill from the Òran Mór to his flat. Doing that was just sort of understood. Although, in saying that, the boys were very drunk by the end of the day and it was never easy. Sometimes, when he was fit, my partner Robert would come down and help push.

And there was a chap called Joe, one of the Jolly Boys, who was in his eighties I think, but who seemed quite fit, absolutely off his head but really nice in that he was the salt-of-the-earth type.

"I'll help you May and the both of us will get him up the road."

So he would help, usually steaming, drunk as a lord, and we would push Alasdair up the hill and up the front steps into the flat. All the while on our uphill trek and steady push with dear old Alasdair singing away. He had a really good voice, he was a tenor. It would usually be something by Ivor Cutler or one of his favourites by Michael Marra. Alasdair loved Michael Marra. So the other day I googled him, and played it and had a wee weep; all I could hear was Alasdair in my head singing *Hermless, Hermless*. Something about him not coming home for his tea. Ever again.

For a man like Alasdair, for any man, having to be in bed for seven was just awful, so what I often did was download a film onto my iPad and we would watch a film together. Alasdair did not own a television. We would drink, me some wine and him a wee whisky. He loved that. Sometimes I would just pop in to make sure everything was good, and we would blether. When he hadn't enjoyed his evening meal, he'd ask if I could get him a fish supper. I'd get it for him and sometimes we'd share.

"Oh and can you pick up a bottle of whisky too, May, while you're out?"

So I would and he'd offer me a tenner for a full bottle of whisky and a fish supper.

"But this is 2019, Alasdair! What decade are you living in!" It was so hilarious. Money was never something he thought about.

He hated being in bed so early (though not quite always as he was easily tired these days) but that's where he had to be because he lived alone, and it took two people to perform this task. I couldn't have managed alone. Being at home was better than being in a care home, which would have happened if his house couldn't have been adapted, enabling him to be at home amongst his books and art supplies.

I should mention, for all I found the Jolly Boys weird about women, George the organiser was nothing if not good to Alasdair. When I was struggling to prepare Alasdair's flat for him to be discharged home from the hospital, George of the Jolly Boys was the sole financial contributor, allowing me to enlist builders' help. He was a godsend. Cheers George!

A man of pen and ink

I can remember one Sunday morning, it would have been around the middle of the morning, generally for most people a time of rest and a bit of idleness. The phone rang. Alasdair had a need. He wanted to send out some emails. Now that is nothing particularly special for most people. Emails are quite straightforward. But Alasdair was engaged in a rear-guard action against the digital age.

Email assistance had been part of my role even back in the days when Morag was still alive, since Morag had finally refused to act as his keyboarder because of the constant changes Alasdair would make to the text. But now, with Morag gone and Alasdair spending more time on his own, there was an increased need for this particular type of help.

On weekdays, over the years, this would have been a task for one of his many paid secretaries or assistants, for Rodge Glass, Stef Gardiner and Helen Lloyd amongst several others, all of whom I had met or got to know when dropping in at Alasdair's home for one reason or another. But at weekends he didn't have an assistant to hand and so that's where I came in. At your service, my dear. We were friends, so no question of payment.

Down the stairs I went and along the Terrace to Number 2. Alasdair was at his desk, in his wheelchair. The computer wasn't switched on.

"Can you switch it on, Alasdair?" He knew where the switch was, but it wasn't easy to reach.

"You do it please May." I obliged.

"And can you enter the password?"

The password was Talisker. He liked the sound of it. For one thing, it was a good whisky and for another it had echoes of his own name. An internal two-syllable rhyme at least.

"No, can you key it in, please May."

"Alasdair, come on, look, let me show you how. Come over to the keyboard. It doesn't bite. You won't get an electric shock."

"I AM NOT TOUCHING THOSE KEYS."

Well, there was no arguing with that tone of voice. I had tried before, but didn't really expect a change in attitude. It wasn't fear, surely. It was simple rejection, a massive NO. I suppose we all have areas of human existence into which we are not prepared to enter. But there can't be many for whom digital rejection is on a par with bungee-jumping or cuddling snakes. So that was that. I entered the password and the computer came to life.

We started the email composition process and after around twenty minutes we had got the first two sentences done.

"Would you like a coffee, May?"

"Thanks. I'll make it."

"Yes, and I'll have an Irish coffee. Two shots of whisky mind and a wee drop of honey."

Forty minutes later and one email was on the verge of completion. Alasdair read it out to himself.

"I don't like that word there," he said, pointing at 'possibly'. Can you please change it to 'perhaps' so that it fits in better with the overall flow and tone."

"Done. See how easy it is to change things."

A simple change. But most times he would dictate the email and then change almost every single word. Delete and start again. Assistants who didn't have the patience of Job would have an issue.

It struck me that maybe there was something in that easiness of changing things that made him reject the whole technology. Tippex and scoring out were much more untidy and cumbersome as methods of deletion or alteration and, in a way, constrained the brain to know what it wanted in the first place. And to stick with it. Did digital text processing threaten the creative flow?

But he was absolutely right in one respect. Emails and the like are prone to disappear, to fade into thin air. Message sent, job done. You can zap it later and free up some space. But letters, of which he wrote me scores and scores, and many of which he headed "unwise letter" (because of the intimate wishes expressed), are much more likely to survive. That's for sure.

The digital rejection extended to mobile phones, although landlines were exempt. He wasn't a hermit after all. Alasdair was never the owner of a mobile phone. When Morag would call him (she did have a mobile and used it quite a lot) when he was out with me or Robert, the call was always to my phone or to Robert's phone, which of course gave him the option of not being there if that was what suited him at the time. Handy.

I remember once asking him about typewriters.

"Surely Alasdair, when you were a young man, you must have wanted a typewriter. Don't all writers sit pecking away at the typewriter keys, making the letters leap up and slap against the paper?"

"I never wanted one. Never ever. I remember watching my father type. But if someone had offered to give me one, then I can say with absolute certainty that I would have had to turn down the offer. They simply did not appeal to me. The whole operation of finding a key and hitting it would have made it impossible for me to write anything at all. I need a pen and ink."

I had to admit that the image of Alasdair Gray sitting pecking away at a typewriter, let alone a computer keyboard or an iPad, tablet or mobile, was just as completely implausible as the image of Alasdair Gray flying a helicopter.

"Are you happy with the wording of this email now, Alasdair?" I asked with some trepidation.

"It's fine. Thank you May. Can you print out a copy for me? One more look." He liked to hold a physical copy.

"Shall I send it?"

"Yes, it can go. But there are two more I want to send."

He sat behind me the whole time, dictating and changing. Sometimes with his head resting on my shoulder. He had some problems holding his head upright, but the end result was not without affection.

So, with Alasdair sitting behind me, the dictating, changing, reconsidering and fine-tuning process would start over again for two more emails.

"Ready to send now, Alasdair?"

"Just let me read them just one more time."

"Of course, sweetie. I'll make another coffee."

"Same again for me, May."

He read. Approvingly.

"OK now?"

"They can go."

It was now the middle of Sunday afternoon (lunch hadn't happened, although the care staff had been and gone) and we had achieved the great task of composing and sending off three emails. In recognition of this, the sun had come out.

In the old days this would have been the time for a tramp in the park. But those days were over.

Gone

Stef called me one morning. He was in an absolute panic.

"May, can you please come down? Quickly. Alasdair's not well."

I ran down to Number 2. Stef was alone there with Alasdair. Gary the carer wasn't there. Alasdair was slumped in his wheelchair by his desk. The colour had completely drained from his face. Lips blue. He was struggling to breathe. I dialled 999 for an ambulance, which arrived within 20 minutes. I climbed into the ambulance with him.

Here we were again, hurtling through the city in the back of an ambulance. I knew this would be our last journey together. I stayed with him until he was admitted to a ward. During this time I phoned his sister, Mora. I would have contacted his son Andrew, but he had never wanted to give me any contact information.

I visited every day. The first family member to arrive was his niece, Katrina. Then Mora. Andrew arrived from America with a few hours to spare.

We sat in the single room, Katrina, Andrew and me with Alasdair breathing his last breaths.

"Andrew, this is no time for ill feeling. I think we should hug."

He sortofdid. I went to the bed and held Alasdair's hand for about twenty minutes. I couldn't stop crying.

"So sorry about your father," said a nurse who came in.

"He's not my dad, he's my friend, but thank you for your care."

"You'll want to be alone with your dad."

Andrew nodded. I left.

The way he was breathing told me

he was almost gone now

gone.

a husk

Aftermath

Alasdair hadn't wanted a funeral. He wanted his body to be left to medical science, to Glasgow University. This had been important to him. It didn't happen. It couldn't happen.

A few days after his death I got a phonecall from Mora inviting me and Florence and Robert to go down to Number 2 for coffee and cake. Katrina was there too. And Andrew. Robert didn't go. Mora and Katrina were talking about which of Alasdair's paintings they wanted for themselves.

"Has Alasdair's body been collected?" I asked in a wee small voice.

"He was cremated yesterday."

CHRIST! Why couldn't someone have let me know! Florence, so loyal, was very upset too.

Who was there at the crematorium? No one? The undertakers came to pick up the body from the hospital mortuary. And he was taken to be cremated.

No ceremony. No mourners present.

He got his wish. No funeral.

++++

"Right, let's get sorting out the contents in this place," said someone.

"Does anyone want this little table?"

"Do we just auction the whole lot?"

"I suppose we just pick the paintings we want."

"May, I can't get into the filing cabinet. Would you mind coming down with some pliers and a hammer?"

I left them picking through the objects in the still living carcass of the flat. The possessions of the dead were all looking at me with Alasdair's eyes.

Loving Alasdair

After Alasdair died, there wasn't a traditional funeral. He had requested that his body be donated to medical science, which wasn't possible. Alasdair's death left a void; I felt like a part of me was missing and I needed what people nowadays would call closure, but I doubt you can ever "close" that chapter in your life when someone you had such an affinity with dies.

Determined to say goodbye in my own way, I decided I'd organise an intimate memorial evening. Initially, I'd considered hosting it at my flat but soon realised that would not work as my flat was too small. I contacted Colin Beattie at the Òran Mór to ask about hiring a space for the event. I wanted to give Alasdair's friends the chance to say their goodbyes and share fond memories of him. To honour his memory and gather those together who cared about and respected him, I created a post about the event on my private Facebook page called *Loving Alasdair* and the Òran Mór posted it too. Colin agreed it would be good to have an evening celebrating what he meant to us and Scotland. The wee night was held on 3 March 2020 and many close friends arrived. Colin showed his support and deep respect for Alasdair by providing fantastic food and making sure there were drinks available.

Many individuals who knew Alasdair well, as well as representatives from local parliamentary constituency offices, attended the event. (I had written to our local MP, Patrick Grady, on the matter of commemoration of a special person.)

I didn't need to be nervous about the night (but I was). I started speaking.

I've named this evening Loving Alasdair, *because I did. I adored him. As I'm also sure many of you did. What initially began as unfulfilled desires on his part evolved into a deep and enduring bond of friendship that lasted until the very end. Tonight is about saying goodbye and remembering him in our own way. You'll know that Alasdair was Glasgow's very own Michelangelo and if you haven't seen the amazing ceiling in the Òran Mór, then you are truly missing out. It's our own Sistine Chapel. Alasdair was an amazing writer, poet, muralist and likely the most socially minded person I've ever known or am ever likely to know.*

But then I deviated from my prepared notes to speak freely. And of course I just had to trot out my well-worn joke about Alasdair and me having first met through the Yellow Pages*. As an addition, I'd approached Mora, Alasdair's sister, to see if she would share some significant childhood memories, and she graciously agreed.

Toward the end of my introduction, my voice began to waver and Liz Kristiansen, a kind woman who'd been a professional newsreader, stepped up to help me out. It was all too much for the microphone as well, which broke down and couldn't be replaced. So we all had to speak up and speaker after speaker told hilarious stories. The stories and reminiscences stretched on for well beyond an hour, and none of it was tedious; in fact, some memories had me laughing hysterically. After food was served, other memories began to surface. I've got a story, I've got a story! And that is what the evening was like, everyone supporting each other.

It was such a good night, a very necessary farewell to a good man.

Here's what Mora said:

* See page 19

Early life with Alasdair.

Alasdair was two years older than me and I only start remembering him when we moved from Glasgow with my mother to avoid the bombing. My Dad stayed in the city working but joined us at weekends. We lived near a farm, where the photograph Alasdair so liked was taken. We could have been going to collect the milk. We also moved to East Kilbride where we lived in a flat opposite the school. The lavatory was in the back yard down a flight of outside stairs. During our stay there my poor mother had a terrible time as both of us caught measles, chicken pox and whooping cough one after the other. I remember lying in the bed in the alcove with the curtains closed. Alasdair started school there.

Next we moved to Wetherby in Yorkshire as my Dad became the manager of a war worker's hostel and so began 3 or 4 years of financial security and as Mum was an excellent house keeper she saved enough to keep us going on our return to Glasgow when the war ended and Dad was unemployed. Our stay in Wetherby was great. We had a wee dog, Sandy, a garden, space to roam and strange to say it was probably the best time for Mum and Dad also. But Alasdair was much more aware of the war than myself and suffered from nightmares and bad eczema. We counted the aeroplanes leaving at night on their bombing trips and also counted them returning. Alasdair joined the church choir as he got paid for attending weddings etc. I went to a ballet class. We walked to the council school together although some folk thought we should be sent to a private school being the manager's children. Alasdair was having trouble with some of the boys at school and my Dad was trying to help him to fight them, with no success. Alasdair was like a windmill flailing around just hoping to hit something. We cycled around the countryside, swam in the river, I remember it as the good times. Dad took Alasdair to the Wetherby horse races where he sat and read a book and never returned as a horse had to be shot after a bad fall, so I was taken instead and loved it.

The return to Glasgow was tricky. Alasdair had to sit his qualifying and we both started the new school with English accents, not acceptable, and Dad was seeking work. I made friends, settled down and began to enjoy life. Alasdair had more trouble adjusting and his asthma attacks caused problems for him also. He would shout bedtime stories across the hallway to me and get very cross the following night when I had to admit I had fallen asleep before he had finished. My Dad tried to take him to football matches but he was not interested so I went along instead. It was the same with climbing hills, I went, Alasdair stayed at home with Mum. Here arguments between us started. He used to draw pictures for me in an old autograph album of Mum's and I treasured it. One day we had an argument and he took a bottle of ink and smeared it over the book. We had to take it in turns to wash or dry dishes. One memorable evening I was out playing in the back green when the kitchen window was thrown open and I saw smoke billowing out. Alasdair had decided it would be quicker to put the cutlery under the grill to dry it but the knife handles caught fire and then one of my Mum's best tea towels was used to quench the flames.

Alasdair always said we were competing for attention and warmth. Our Aunt and Uncle used to come over from the south side to spend time with us and we would play paper and pencil games like Telegrams and Consequences. Alasdair was always so much better than myself and I did not enjoy the games much. We had our own friends and it was on our summer holidays that we spent most time together. We would rent a house on Millport or Arran for a month and we so enjoyed it. Wet days were spent painting, reading and playing games, dry days were spent making dens. Mum became ill with cancer when I was 14. I was not told she was dying and it was Alasdair who stayed *beside her, brushed her hair, kept her company. After she died life changed. When both of us were eventually attending college, Alasdair at the Glasgow School of Art and myself at Dunfermline College of Physical Education, I chose to concentrate on the only subject I was good at and that Alasdair could not attempt, we became good friends and that is how it remained.*

but me

I

remember   remember

so much

remember one night

when I walked in with Alasdair they didn't have time to stop holding hands we saw them Morag and her man but all he did was look over at them annoyed and you could see the anger on his face but he said absolutely nothing I know but he would get really annoyed sometimes because he knew he knew and said nothing always coming in the side door of Tennent's bar not the main door because that way he could see them sat in their corner and avoid a confrontation he could sneakily look over at them from that angle and all the bar staff were following this soap but she would never have let those vultures into the flat when the poor man too kind for his own good would let them give him a whisky because he couldn't stand up to get the bottle and sign a few paintings or drawings over to them for next to nothing because he liked to be generous and nae concerns for his ain interests with those two guys who came in and ushered wee Florence out the room so they could have a chat like with the man himself but wee Morag would have had none of that the feisty wee bampot she wouldn't but she was gone and not there to ignore him and protect him oh how shall I describe him you don't need a code to see him you know I have to get this cuddly red lobster to Alasdair up there on the scaffolding sorry health and safety strictly forbids the presence of any form of crustacean on scaffolding but it will make him happy oh can't you walk a little faster I can't bloody walk at all at all at all do you know Andrew grabbed the phone off him and wouldn't let me carry on the call and all I wanted was just to talk about the next film I was going to take down to him vulnerable lovely man which we were going to watch on my iPad when his son had gone back to America you'll be speaking to me not my father I'm not going to hang up Andrew you need to let me speak to your dad no I'm not going to do that then I will just need to come around I'm just a few doors away I was I was shaking with nerves then somehow Alasdair got the phone back I'm really sorry for Andrew's behaviour his voice all trembling all vulnerable not understanding or did he why does his son hate me why why what have I done well the expression of love can take the strangest forms and the desire to protect turns itself into anger ha ha ha like Bella Baxter said you never can be kind because you are afraid afraid but not your dad how shall I describe thee dirty-minded generous lovely soul George saw you in the bushes with Morag at the People's Palace you rutting Gray and all those letters you wrote me my God you didn't hold back at all did you the Eternal Feminine has got you in her claws her gorgeous claws and why do you always pour all the different drinks into just one glass oh editor speaking Mr Gray if you will insist on adding spurious and incorrect annotations and amendments in order to confuse or as you doubtless suppose to entertain amuse and titivate the poor things reading your interminable stuff then enough enough oh how shall I describe thee lovely non-digital man did you not once take flying lessons or was I dreaming must have been dreaming it all so Mr Gray or may I call you Alasdair this stick controls upwards and downwards motion and this one lets you move to the right or to the left like so yes just like that you've got it so your passengers are ready to go now take them up for a low-level flight over your lovely city over the Glaswegian green the Glaswegian grey the Glaswegian red and yellow sandstone and grid patterns and elegant curves and of course the thundering endlessly droning motorway oh how shall I describe thee off you go away you go now away away

Acknowledgements

I have several people to thank who helped me in writing this memoir. For giving me permission to use their letters I must thank Ulrike Seeberger, my niece Jennifer McKnight and Mora Rolley, Alasdair's sister. My partner Robert was an invaluable supporter and suffered me pestering him for little details. There were several friends in the West End of Glasgow who encouraged me, in particular Colin Beattie and George Tomlinson. My thanks also to Elfreda Crehan for designing and putting the files together and also for transcribing my audio files. Especially I want to thank Peter Terrell who edited the book, fitted all the various pieces together in a contributory sort of way, kept me on the right track, made me suffer by making me bring up my memories and always insisted that the truth matters.

also from VOICES

V
clamavi

To This Northern Shore

Pieces of a life
from
South to North

A MEMOIR

Jean-Luc Barbanneau

VOICES

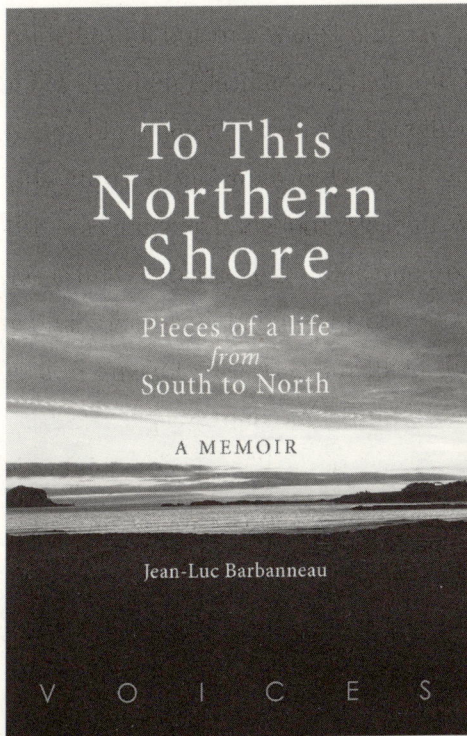

I found it flowing, engaging and
charmingly honest! I loved the gentle
yet deep reflective spirit throughout.
I also had a good laugh!

C.C. ~ Oxford